TRIAL
of
FAITH
*Religion and Politics
in Tocqueville's Thought*

TRIAL
of
FAITH

Religion and Politics
in Tocqueville's Thought

Doris S. Goldstein

ELSEVIER

New York / Oxford / Amsterdam

ELSEVIER SCIENTIFIC PUBLISHING COMPANY, INC.
52 Vanderbilt Avenue, New York, N.Y. 10017

ELSEVIER SCIENTIFIC PUBLISHING COMPANY
335 Jan Van Galenstraat, P.O. Box 211
Amsterdam, The Netherlands

Library of Congress Cataloging in Publication Data

Goldstein, Doris S
  Trial of faith.

  Bibliography: p.
  Includes index.
  1. Christianity and politics—History.
2. France—Religion.   3. France—Politics and
government.   4. United States—Religion.   5. Religions.   6. Tocqueville, Alexis Charles Henri
Maurice Clérel de, 1805–1859.   I. Title.
BR115.P7G59   209'.44   75-4753
ISBN O-444-99001-1

Manufactured in the United States of America

To the memory of Koppel S. Pinson

Contents

Preface

Perhaps the most enduring tribute to the richness and vitality of Tocqueville's thought is the fact that there remain within it unexplored areas and meaningful problems. The purpose of this study is to chart one of these areas, that of religion. Both Tocqueville's major works and his correspondence testify to his continued interest in religious phenomena and their social and political ramifications. This interest has been noted by biographers, historians, and social scientists, some of whom have advanced varying interpretations of the role of religion in Tocqueville's life and thought. There has, however, been no sustained scrutiny and analysis.

Such scrutiny must be guided by the awareness that Tocqueville's interest in religion was deeply personal and yet animated by the concerns of "the man of knowledge." Therefore, it is important to begin with biographical data, and to explore the relationship between Tocqueville's personal attitudes and those insights and theoretical formulations pertinent to the historian and the social scientist. This approach is not meant to insinuate a kind of psychological or historical reductionism: I assume that the value of ideas must be decided independently of their psychological or historical origins. In short, the purpose of linking Tocqueville's personal life to his theories is understanding, not dismissal.

If the facts of biography provide one set of landmarks for the historian in search of that terra firma definable as Tocqueville's religious position, another may be found by reference to nine-teenth-century French society and politics. Because he saw himself as an *homme politique* rather than as a closet philosopher, the political and social circumstances of his own country were not only the context, but the catalyst, of both thought and action. Nowhere is this more evident than in his concern with those vexing problems involving religion and politics that agitated French society. His efforts to understand these problems, and to arrive at solutions to them, were the very substance out of which his more general theories were created. Consequently, if explication of Tocqueville's views about religion is not to become an arid and disembodied exercise, it must be rooted in the facts of French history and politics.

By pulling out one thread from the fabric of a man's life and thought and subjecting it to intensive examination, one risks the danger of substituting the part for the whole, of exaggerating the importance of one idea or cluster of ideas. The reader will judge the extent to which this kind of distortion has been avoided. However, I assume that Tocqueville's thought consists of a network of inter-connected themes, with no fixed order of primacy among them. I propose to show that those ideas that can be grouped under the rubric of religion constitute a distinct and pervasive theme, which is significantly related to other motifs. And, since Tocqueville was an historian and theorist of uncommon stature, these ideas merit attention apart from their relevance to his life and work. But attention need not imply inflated claims, and hopefully this book will further that enterprise of critical evaluation which appears finally to have supplanted adulation in discussions of Alexis de Tocqueville.

I should like to thank Edward T. Gargan, André Jardin, Arno J. Mayer, and Melvin Richter for their assistance, advice, and sundry kindnesses. The American Association of University Women and the American Council of Learned Societies provided financial aid that helped me to complete the research for this book, and the Frederick Lewis Allen Room of the New York Public Library extended its hospitality. To these institutions I wish to express my appreciation.

TRIAL
of
FAITH

Religion and Politics
in Tocqueville's Thought

George Wilson Pierson, doyen of American Tocqueville studies, has been unfailingly generous and helpful. His interest in my work has been enormously encouraging, and has extended to the careful reading of the manuscript, the search for a title, and acute suggestions and comments. To say that I am grateful is an understatement that must suffice.

My obligations to Felix Gilbert are difficult to express in brief compass. It was he who originally suggested that I work on Tocqueville, and from the inception of this book to the final reading of the manuscript I have benefited from his awesome learning and critical acumen. To have studied with Felix Gilbert is to have had the opportunity of discovering the depth and nuance of which historical scholarship is capable. I should like to pay homage to his influence and example.

Doris S. Goldstein

New York City
September 1974

Chapter I

The Problem of Personal Religious Belief

The nature of an individual's religious beliefs is sometimes easily established, either because of explicit statements or because certain lifelong patterns of thought and behavior readily reveal themselves. This is not so in the case of Tocqueville: he was reticent, and rarely discussed personal matters, even with his family and closest friends. As a result, there is a relative paucity of information. Nor does the available material permit simple and unambiguous classifications. There is no alternative, then, to probing an inherently delicate subject. The relationship between Tocqueville's personal religious beliefs and his views as an historian and theorist is both close and complex: therefore the former cannot remain unexamined.

Understanding of the nature of Tocqueville's religious commitments must begin with the realization that family background and early education linked him, not to the France of the Revolution, but to the France of aristocracy, monarchy, and Catholicism. By ancestry he belonged to the Norman nobility, the son of a family that had retained its traditional loyalty to the Church as well as to the Monarchy. He was brought up amid pervasive memories of the old regime, surrounded by relatives and friends of his own class, and educated by a priest long attached to the Tocqueville family.[1] There is ample evidence that Tocqueville felt deep affection and respect for this priest, the Abbé Lesueur, whose example and teachings must have served to bind his pupil to the traditional faith.[2] Traces of this early environment remained, and help to explain what John Stuart Mill described as Tocqueville's tendency

1

to cling to the past, especially with respect to religion.[3]

But the carefully constructed barriers that had surrounded his childhood began to crumble when Tocqueville, at the age of fifteen, left his home to attend the lycée at Metz. His peers were no longer limited to the offspring of the aristocracy, and at the lycée he formed an enduring friendship with Eugène Stoffels. It was not similarity of birth, position, or even intellectual interests that united the two young men, but rather—significantly—Tocqueville's recognition of Stoffel's "moral worth."[4] While at Metz he also experienced a religious crisis, forcing him for the first time to question the teachings of the Church.[5] Aware of his erstwhile pupil's growing estrangement from family values and traditions, the worried Abbé Lesueur gently warned Tocqueville not to allow himself to be infected by "the spirit of the times," and to avoid bad company and bad books.[6] Two years later, after he had left Metz and was studying law in Paris, Tocqueville admitted to Lesueur: "I believe, but I cannot practice."[7] Ambiguous though it is, this remark confirms the impression that Tocqueville was moving away from the certitudes of the milieu in which he had been born and raised.

From 1823 until his visit to America in 1831 much of Tocqueville's time was spent at Paris studying law and then at Versailles, where he held a judicial position. During these years he evinced a growing interest in politics and history, which was reinforced by his new-found friendship with Gustave de Beaumont.* And the explosive political situation of the last years of the Restoration, together with exposure to new ideas, was gradually channeling these interests into a hesitant sympathy for political liberalism. There is some evidence that he belonged to the *Société* de la *morale chrétienne*, an organization that constituted the liberal reply to the Ultra religious and political views of the *Congrégation*.[8] Attendance at Guizot's lectures on the "History of Civilization in France" was another symptom of interest in the liberal interpretation of French history and politics.[9] Tocqueville's letters of 1829 and 1830 were openly critical of the blindness and intransigeance of the Ultras, and especially of the Polignac ministry itself. In one of the most interesting of these letters he wrote that instead of fighting "the irresistible tendencies of the century," the

*It may be as well to note explicitly that the subject of religion is not one of those which is amenable to "collective study" of Tocqueville and Beaumont. (See Seymour Drescher, *Tocqueville and Beaumont on Social Reform* [New York, 1968], pp. 201-217, for a cogent argument in behalf of "collective study.") The personal, one might say the temperamental, attitudes of the two men towards religion were very different, and this difference is sometimes reflected in the positions they took on French religious issues.

2

government should attempt to work with them, first and foremost by disconnecting religion from politics.[10]

Evidences of a turn towards political liberalism, and of dissatisfaction with Restoration church–state relationships, do not in themselves reveal anything about the development of Tocqueville's personal religious beliefs. Aside from the fact that a chance reading of eighteenth-century literature sparked a religious crisis in 1820, very little is known about the impingement of external influences upon his religious life. Whether, or to what extent, the literature and speculation of the Restoration helped to shape his religious, as well as his political views, remains a matter of speculation. G. W. Pierson has noted the similarity of some of Tocqueville's attitudes to the Romantic "mal de siècle," and there are other affinities to ideas current in nineteenth-century France.[11] Nevertheless, the study of external influences is not the most promising approach to the clarification of Tocqueville's religious position. One discovers that to a far greater extent than might be expected in dealing with an *érudit*, this position derived from a few premises, barely articulated but strongly felt, and ultimately from his own temperament and personality. To uncover these premises, which underwent no perceptible change throughout his life, is therefore of the first importance. Some suggestive influences and affinities will also incidentally reveal themselves, but they are possibilities rather than certainties.

Tocqueville's most pronounced characteristic appears to have been a kind of moral earnestness, a conviction that life was "a serious matter" in which human beings had the obligation to render the best possible account of themselves.[12] He made strenuous moral and spiritual demands upon himself, analyzed his motives and actions with a scrupulousness worthy of his seventeenth-century compatriots of Port-Royal, and was somewhat self-consciously "serious," "upright," "earnest." In all of these qualities he resembled Guizot, and it is not surprising that during the July Monarchy both men were mocked upon the Parisian stage for their moralizing inclinations.[13] But, while outwardly "austere and sober," to cite his friend Ampère's description, Tocqueville was always inwardly troubled by restlessness and discontent.[14] This was caused partially by frustration at his own inability to attain those heights of achievement and excellence to which he aspired. More than that, and this is mentioned again and again in his letters, there was a sense of the world itself, and especially the times in which he lived, somehow falling short of his ideals.[15] This last point is a possible link between Tocqueville and the Romantics, for he was as

3

conscious as a Vigny or a Musset of having been born into a time that was out of joint. What is certain is that Tocqueville's emotional makeup was that of an idealist, if this word is defined in its garden variety sense of one whose behavior and thought is guided by belief in, and aspiration towards, some set of absolutes.

But in Tocqueville's mind idealism, or a taste for "great deeds and noble qualities" was automatically identified with a "spiritual" outlook.[16] Hence, praise of the "spiritual" and disdain of the "material" were ubiquitous in his writings, although it was not always clear exactly what meanings these terms were intended to express.[17] The bourgeois of the July Monarchy, in his self-seeking quest for financial gain, was tarred with "materialism," but so too was the Revolution of 1848, because it had its origins partially "in the stomach of the nation," in "the taste for material pleasures."[18] Sainte-Beuve caught the callousness to which this somewhat overstretched idealism could lead, when he replied that "there is nothing more respectable than the stomach, no cry which speaks louder than that of poverty."[19] Any theory that Tocqueville considered to be a form of materialism fell under the same wholesale anathema: the historical theories of Buckle, all racial theories, and even Hegelianism, because the latter gave rise to anti-Christian and antispiritual philosophies.[20] Frequently, his mode of argument tended to confound belief that these theories were false, with the judgment that they were "pernicious," "a dangerous disease of the human mind."[21] Nevertheless, there can be no doubt of his conviction that all theories that would make men into creatures at the mercy of race, geography, or other purely material considerations were gross perversions of human nature. This emerged most clearly in those superb letters to Gobineau in which Tocqueville rejected the philosophy of the *Essai sur l'inégalité des races humaines.* He maintained that moral choice did exist, that men were capable of nonmaterial aspirations and conduct. Precisely for this reason were they worthy of respect rather than of scorn.[22] Many years earlier, while pondering these same questions, he had arrived at the conclusion that human beings were instinctively drawn towards ideal values. The proof was that throughout the centuries the books that exercised the greatest influence were those that taught "the beautiful and the good, the lofty and beneficial theories of the existence of God and the immortality of the soul."[23] Because he never abandoned this belief, his contempt for materialism, although tinged with a certain callousness, did not lead to self-righteousness. Far from being wrapped up in contemplation of his own highminded nature, Tocqueville believed that he and his fellow

4

men shared the common capacity—and obligation—to strive towards the highest possible spiritual and moral goals.

In the passage cited above, Tocqueville linked devotion to "the beautiful and the good" with belief in God and the immortality of the soul. This was no casual remark, for it reflected his assumption that any Weltanschauung that emphasized the spiritual rather than the material was necessarily inseparable from religion. He did not find emotional or intellectual sustenance in systems of secular idealism, and he considered philosophical speculation to be idle and fruitless. Only religion could provide a sound basis for idealism, because it inculcated belief in the soul and its immortality, and thereby drew men away from undue preoccupation with material goods and interests.[24] This was a matter of personal belief, but to Tocqueville it was also a generalization about human nature. He was, in addition, echoing a sentiment frequently expressed in nineteenth-century France: religion was that instinct in man that led to awareness of a supermundane reality.[25] Similarly, his repeated assertion that religion was the sole means through which fundamental ethical and philosophical questions could be answered must be construed on three different levels: certainly it was an expression of his personal needs and values, but it was also a psychological and sociological generalization, and one very much in keeping with the vague religiosity of the period in which he lived.

The salient point is, as John Stuart Mill perceived, that Tocqueville was not a secular, highminded rationalist whose interest in religion could be divorced from personal factors. He did not feel himself to be exempt from what he regarded as the common human need for religious belief, did not look upon unbelief as a breaking of shackles, a liberation into the world of free thought. And yet, in 1820 his own faith was shaken by a chance exposure to irreligious literature. In a letter written many years later he described the shock and suffering caused by this experience in terms that vividly illuminate his previous depth of belief.[26] Although this may have been merely a temporary adolescent religious crisis, his private papers suggest that he was never able to regain those firm and fixed religious convictions that he so earnestly desired. Again and again he revealed his longing for the serene faith with which he had been imbued, the misery of doubt, and his regret that "I am not a believer."[27]

What, then, was Tocqueville able to salvage out of the disintegration of his former unquestioned Catholicism? Careful examination of the source material, despite numerous lacunae, does make it possible to go beyond the statement that he was "religious" in some vaguely defined sense. For example, he unequivocally expressed his belief in the doctrine of the immortality of the soul, writing that he was convinced that the injustices and inconsistencies of this world would be rectified in another.[28] He also mentioned the consolation that belief in an afterlife afforded to human beings, at one point stating baldly that, "After all, only religion can teach one how to die."[29] There was no suggestion that he accepted the doctrine of the immortality of the soul as a divinely revealed dogma. It was rather in his own nature that he found irrefutable proof of its validity: he as a human being rebelled against the possibility that there is no ultimate judgment of good and evil. He held that man needed belief in an afterlife to endure the knowledge of death with courage and nobility, and he argued that the very need for the infinite in human beings was proof of the immortality of the soul.[30] Released from dogmatic adherence to Catholicism by the inroads of doubt, he looked to the psychological realities of human existence for verification of one of its most basic principles. In so doing, he was not only merging personal views with assumptions about "man's" feelings and needs, but he was also merging "truth" with "utility."

One of the strongest ties that bound Tocqueville to Christianity was veneration of its spiritual and ethical qualities. Only in the Gospel did he find the kind of aspiration "which gives rise to a larger and purer moral atmosphere.[31] This constituted the essential difference, not only between paganism and Christianity, but between Christianity and the Eastern higher religions. His evaluations of Islam and Hinduism were, in large part, variations upon the theme of the moral and spiritual superiority of Christianity. The fact that the teachings of the Gospel were able to inspire a pure and ethical life was an ultimate test for Tocqueville.[32] Conversely, he was contemptuous of those who called themselves good Christians, although their particular sort of religion did not deter them from evil and violence. The pseudoreligiosity of the early years of the Second Empire produced many such "Christians," provoking Tocqueville to exclaim: "Be rather pagans of guiltless behavior, proud souls and clean hands, than Christians of this type."[33] Although this outburst should not be taken quite literally, it does point out the extent to which he correlated Christian belief with ethical behavior. When he learned that the first volume of Buckle's *History of Civilisation in England* had been enthusiastically received, he was astonished and indignant. How could the English, with their "religious habits," acclaim the work of this "anti-Christian" materialist?[34] To Tocqueville, belief in Christianity ought surely to result in aversion to ideas incompatible with the Christian conception of human nature and conduct.

Both philosophical and theological speculation were, he thought, arid exercises, no more and sometimes less satisfactory than common sense in explaining the "why" of the world. It was in Revelation that he found the clearest ideas about the origin and purpose of the world, free will and responsibility.[35] His philosophical position was indeed akin to that of Christianity. Belief in a First Cause provided the foundation; thence he moved on to acceptance of,

> . . . fixed laws which can be seen in the physical world and which it is necessary to admit in the moral world; the providence of God and therefore His justice; the responsibility of human beings for their actions, since they have been allowed knowledge of the existence of good and evil, and, consequently, of an afterlife.[36]

This passage, written a year before his death, provides a succinct statement of Tocqueville's religious and philosophical outlook. It expresses his acceptance of what he regarded as the simple and obvious truths of religion, truths that were at the heart of Christianity itself. Neither in this letter nor elsewhere did he declare his adherence to any of the specifically theological doctrines of Catholic Christianity. Without question, his faith, respect, and veneration were reserved for the Gospel. But, according to his own interpretation, the Gospel "speaks only of the general relations of men to God and to each other, beyond which it inculcates and imposes no point of faith."[37]

There have been various attempts to prove that during the last decade of his life Tocqueville's religious doubts were resolved, and that he ended his life a convinced Catholic. For example, it has been alleged that Beaumont tampered with or suppressed evidence that would prove that Tocqueville returned to the Catholic faith. A grave accusation, and one that appears to rest largely upon a misconstrual of Beaumont's motives in opposing publication of one of Tocqueville' letters.[38] Although it is undeniable that Beaumont did not exercise his responsibilities as editor of his friend's unpublished papers with the scrupulousness that modern scholarship has come to expect, the editor of the superb new edition of the Tocqueville–Beaumont correspondence has concluded that Beaumont's additions and deletions did not result in distortion of Tocqueville's ideas. Nowhere does he state, or even hint, that Beaumont wished to give a misleading impression of Tocqueville's religious views.[39] After the latter's death Beaumont's public stance was in fact the same as that of other friends and of family members: Tocqueville had lived and died as a Christian.[40] All

7

were animated by the desire to preserve the proprieties, and all restricted themselves to part of the truth while avoiding problems and ambiguities.

The fact that Tocqueville apparently died as a Catholic, asking for and receiving extreme unction, is the most telling argument in favor of the contention that he returned to the Church. On the other hand, there is evidence that his acceptance of the last rites owed much to secular considerations, and did not constitute an act of faith in Catholic doctrines.[41] The crux of the matter is really that delicate question of the relationship between external observance and personal convictions, a question that impinges upon the realm of the theologian and the psychologist.* Insofar as the available accounts provide some guide to the motivations of a dying man, the most probable interpretation is that Tocqueville took the last sacrament, despite his reservations about Catholic doctrine, because he felt close enough to what he considered the essence of Christianity to be able to affirm his communion with that Christian Church into which he had been born. We cannot weigh the relative importance of the religious and secular influences that impelled him to make this decision. In any case, the matter of Tocqueville's last religious acts is not of central importance to the historian, since these acts are not necessarily a reliable guide to the ideas and beliefs that he held throughout his life.

Discussions of Tocqueville's religious beliefs have frequently become mired in verbal confusions, in which the words "religious," "Christian," and "Catholic" are used as though they were interchangeable. In terms of the question of his relationship to Catholicism, this has meant that evidence of Tocqueville's belief in the immortality of the soul, his adherence to Christian ethical and philosophical doctrines, and his respect for the Church itself, are adduced as proofs of convinced Catholicism.[42] Others have seen only the early loss of Catholic faith and have ignored Tocqueville's continued personal concern with religion and his residual Christian beliefs.[43] This makes him far too secular a thinker, and neglects the connections between his personal religious beliefs and his historical and theoretical statements about religion. If to be "religious" is to believe in a Deity whose existence gives the world order and meaning, then Tocqueville was religious. From the existence of God he derived belief in a moral and

---

*Probably Tocqueville's attitude towards religious faith vis-à-vis religious observance can best be understood in terms of Pascal, who recommended "des gestes de la foi" as a means of attaining faith. For both men doubt or unbelief was a misfortune. Therefore, to seek faith through deeds and observances was wholly acceptable.

8

physical order, in the immortality of the soul, and in the human capacity for free and responsible action. Even though his reasons for accepting these precepts were frequently couched in terms of "need" and "utility," he did accept them. He found both the need and the justification for religious belief within himself, and assumed that these were characteristics of human nature in general. Thus, his functional approach to religious phenomena or, as Tocqueville himself described it, his tendency to consider religion "from a human point of view," rested ultimately upon conclusions that he had drawn from introspection.

The historian of ideas will trace this mode of thought to the Enlightenment, and especially to Montesquieu, whose disciple Tocqueville was, in this respect as in so many others.[44] Possibly Tocqueville was also influenced by those among his contemporaries who affirmed that religion was an innate feeling or instinct in man. This view was shared by individuals as diverse as the liberal Constant, the sometime Ultra Chateaubriand, the eclectic philosopher Cousin, as well as by many of the Romantic poets. In the absence of evidence, this remains a matter of speculation. Nor is the question one of the first importance, since what may be descibed as the new religiosity attempted to exorcise the spectre of religious doubt by methods that had more in common with the Enlightenment than with Christian apologetics. That is, the grounds for belief continued to be those of individual feeling and need. After influences and affinities have been duly noted, however, the crucial point is Tocqueville's innate "feeling" or "need" for religion. In what other way can his acceptance of these arguments by explained? Loss of the religious certitudes of his youth meant that his own intellect and feelings became the criteria of validity: this did not imply atheism, or even agnosticism, but rather adherence to a loose set of nondoctrinal beliefs.

Whether Tocqueville should be described as "Christian" on the basis of these beliefs is essentially a matter of nomenclature. Unquestionably, he thought in terms of the God revealed in the Gospel, and of the basic philosophical and ethical tenets of Christianity. There is an intriguing note, written while Tocqueville was in America, in which he remarked that the teachings of Christianity were compatible with the rationalism of Descartes and of the eighteenth century.[45] But he was unconcerned with the doctrinal differences that separated the various Christian Churches. This dislike of sectarianism persisted throughout his adult life and reached an apogee during the Second Empire, as a result of the obsequious attitude of the "dévots" towards Louis Napoleon.[46] It was Sainte-Beuve who suggested the

9

truth in all its simplicity, when he wrote that Tocqueville continued to believe in "a portion of Christianity": namely, the existence of God, spirituality, and the immortality of the soul.[47] This was indeed the essence of Tocqueville's faith.

To conclude on this note would be to present too facile and systematic an account, obscuring the fact that his ambiguous relationship to Catholicism caused Tocqueville much distress. He had, after all, been born and educated in a thoroughly Catholic milieu and had retained affection and respect for the Church throughout his life. But affection and respect are not synonymous with belief. When Tocqueville confessed to Gobineau that he was an "unbeliever" who was far from priding himself on his unbelief, he was admitting his inability to accept Catholic doctrine and his regret for his lost faith.[48] Just two years before his death he acknowledged his esteem for those who were capable of wholehearted acceptance of Catholicism, writing that this road was not open to all who sought it, ". . . and many who are sincerely searching for it have not yet had the happiness of discovering it."[49] A personal, almost wistful, quality is evident as he explains that there are many who have the utmost respect and veneration for Catholicism without "unfortunately" being completely convinced.[50]

Why was he unable to attain this kind of conviction? Why was he unable, throughout his adult life, to recover those beliefs that he had held before his youthful loss of faith? Ultimately, one cannot know. What does appear beyond question is that his encounter with eighteenth-century thought had a permanent effect. For him, as for so many others, Cartesianism and its eighteenth-century offspring had disclosed an apparent incompatibility between faith and reason. Not all of Christian teaching was undermined, but now adherence to—or recovery of—Catholic belief could come about only through a "leap of faith." Without this, only the most basic Christian ethical and philosophical precepts remained proof against the inroads of Cartesian rationalism. And Tocqueville's temperament did not allow him either to rest content with this basic Christianity or to resolve his doubts about Catholic doctrine through faith and faith alone.

Thus it was that religion was for him a tormenting problem, a source of anxiety and dissatisfaction. His rigorous analysis of his own religious limitations, as well as his horror of doubt and unbelief, are reminiscent of Pascal.[51] He aspired to the kind of communion with the personal God of Christianity that Pascal so movingly described, but that Tocqueville was unable to achieve. For him there was no analogue to Pascal's experience of

November 1654, except possibly during his last days. Hence, his religious beliefs—as distinct from his religious desires—remained closer to Montesquieu and the eighteenth-century tradition. Because of this tension between beliefs and aspirations it is impossible to fit Tocqueville's personal views into any simple or rigid categories. His religious outlook can be understood only in its own terms, with its few certainties and many ambiguities. To realize that, in his personal life, religion was a "trial" in many senses of that word, is to begin to comprehend why, as an historian and theorist, Tocqueville was led to fix his attention upon religious phenomena.

Notes

1. The best accounts of Tocqueville's early years, using materials that have since become unavailable, are to be found in George Wilson Pierson, *Tocqueville and Beaumont in America* (New York, 1938), ch. II, and Antoine Redier, *Comme disait M. de Tocqueville* (Paris, 1925), pp. 28–35.

2. The depth of Tocqueville's attachment to the Abbé Lesueur appears most clearly in letters written to his family after the Abbé's death. (See Tocqueville to Edouard de Tocqueville, Sept. 10 and Sept. 12, 1831; Tocqueville to Comtesse de Tocqueville, Sept. 27, 1831.) These letters are in the Beaumont edition of the *Oeuvres complètes* (Paris, 1860–1866), VII, pp. 58–76. Hereafter this edition will be referred to as *Oeuvres* (B), while the new Mayer edition (Paris, 1951–) will be referred to as *Oeuvres* (M). For some sense of the kindliness of the Abbé, and of the closeness of his relationship to Tocqueville, see the Lesueur letters in the Yale Tocqueville Collection, under the rubric A.IV. Hereafter this Collection will be cited as Y.T.Mss.

3. Mill to Tocqueville, Dec. 15, 1856, *Oeuvres* (M), Tome VI *(Correspondance anglaise)*, p. 350.

4. Beaumont, "Notice sur Alexis de Tocqueville," *Oeuvres* (B), V, pp. 101–102.

5. Pierson, op. cit., p. 17; Redier, op. cit., pp. 38–39, 287–288.

6. Lesueur to Tocqueville, July 16, 1822, Y. T. Mss., A.IV.

7. Tocqueville to Lesueur, Sept. 8, 1824, cited in Pierson, op. cit., p. 17, note.

8. See Ferdinand-Dreyfus, *L'Assistance sous la Seconde République* (Paris, 1907), pp. 10–11, and Charles Pouthas, *Guizot pendant la Restauration* (Paris, 1923), pp. 342–349.

9. Pierson, op. cit., p. 23.

10. Tocqueville to Charles Stoffels, Apr. 21, 1830, Y. T. Mss, A.VII. See also Tocqueville to Edouard de Tocqueville, Aug. 9, 1829, Apr. 6, 1830, May 6, 1830, *Oeuvres* (B), VI, pp. 3–6, 17–22; Tocqueville to Charles Stoffels, Apr. 21, 1830, Y. T. Mss, A.VII.

11. Pierson, op. cit., p. 743, note.

12. Tocqueville to Charles ___, Oct. 22, 1831, *Oeuvres* (B), VII, pp. 80–84.

Tocqueville's correspondent was probably Charles Stoffels.

13. Douglas Johnson, *Guizot* (London and Toronto, 1963), p. 85.

14. Ampère, "Appendice," *Oeuvres* (M), Tome XI *(Correspondance d'Alexis de Tocqueville avec P. P. Royer-Collard et avec J. -J. Ampère)*, p. 447.

15. Tocqueville to Charles ___, Oct. 22, 1831, *Oeuvres* (B), VII, pp. 81–82; Tocqueville to Kergolay, March 21, 1838, *Oeuvres* (B), V, p. 354; Tocqueville to Mme. Swetchine, Feb. 26, 1857, cited in Redier, op. cit., p. 282; in addition, see the entire correspondence with Royer-Collard, *Oeuvres* (M), Tome XI (op. cit.), pp. 9–122.

16. Tocqueville to Mme. Swetchine, Feb. 26, 1857, cited in Redier, op cit., p. 282.

17. In a notebook entry dealing with patriotism, for example, the following typical passage is to be found: "Tout ce ébranle le coeur humain et l'appelle au-delà des intérêts matériels de la vie et l'élève au-dessus de la peur de la mort est une grande chose." Y. T. Mss, C.Vk, Paquet No. 7, Cahier 1, p. 14.

18. Tocqueville to Bouchitté, May 1, 1848, *Oeuvres* (B), VII, pp. 235–236.

19. Sainte-Beuve, *Nouveaux Lundis* (Paris, 1868), X, p. 317.

20. Y. T. Mss, C.Vk, Paquet No. 7, Cahier 1, p. 37; Tocqueville to Corcelle, July 22, 1854, *Oeuvres* (B), VI, pp. 260–261; Tocqueville to Edward Childe, July 19, 1858, cited in *Quelques correspondants de Mr. et Mrs. Childe* (London, 1912), pp. 75–76. James T. Schleifer has recently pointed out that Tocqueville's personal convictions led him to reject the view that material factors—geography and race—had exercised a determining influence in American development. (See Schleifer, "The Making of Tocqueville's *Democracy:* Studies in the Development of Alexis de Tocqueville's Work on America with Particular Attention to His Sources, His Ideas, and His Methods," unpublished diss., Yale, 1972, pp. 112, 172.)

21. Tocqueville, *Oeuvres* (M), Tome I *(De la démocratie en Amérique)*, vol. 2, p. 151.

22. Tocqueville to Gobineau, Oct. 11, 1853, Nov. 17, 1853, Jan. 8, 1856, Jan. 24, 1857, *Oeuvres* (M), Tome IX *(Correspondance d'Alexis de Tocqueville et d'Arthur de Gobineau)*, pp. 199–204, 244–246, 276–281.

23. Tocqueville to Beaumont, Apr. 22, 1838, *Oeuvres* (M), Tome VIII *(Correspondance d'Alexis de Tocqueville et de Gustave de Beaumont)*, vol. 1, p. 292.

24. Tocqueville to Charles ___, Oct. 22, 1831; Tocqueville to Bouchitté, Jan. 8, 1858; Tocqueville to Beckwith, Sept. 7, 1858, *Oeuvres* (B), VII, pp. 83–84, 476, 511.

25. D. G. Charlton, *Secular Religions in France, 1815-1870* (London, 1963), pp. 28-33.

26. Tocqueville to Mme. Swetchine, Feb. 26, 1857, cited in Redier, op. cit., pp. 287–288.

27. The quotation is from Tocqueville to Gobineau, Oct. 2, 1843, *Oeuvres* (M), Tome IX (op. cit.), p. 57; Tocqueville to Kergolay, June 25, 1834, *Oeuvres* (B), V, p. 322; Tocqueville to Corcelle, Aug. 1, 1850, *Oeuvres* (B), VI, p. 152; Tocqueville to Mme. Swetchine, Feb. 26, 1857, cited in Redier, op cit., p. 288; Y. T. Mss, C.Va, Paquet No. 8, p. 41.

28. Tocqueville to Edouard de Tocqueville, Sept. 10, 1831, *Oeuvres* (B), VII, p. 61; Tocqueville to Mme. Swetchine, Dec. 29, 1856, *Oeuvres* (B), VI, p. 360.

29. The quotation is from Tocqueville to Comtesse de Grancey, Oct. 4, 1835, *Oeuvres* (B), VII, p. 143; also Tocqueville to Bouchitté, Jan. 15, 1836, *Oeuvres* (B), VII, pp. 146–147.

30. Y. T. Mss, C.Va, Paquet No. 8, p. 57.

31. Tocqueville to Gobineau, Oct. 2, 1843, *Oeuvres* (M), Tome IX (op. cit.), p. 57.

32. Ibid., 57–59; Tocqueville to Kergolay, March 21, 1838, *Oeuvres* (B), V, p. 355; Tocqueville to Corcelle, June 18, 1856, *Oeuvres* (B), VI, p. 310.

33. Tocqueville to Gobineau, Jan. 24, 1857, *Oeuvres* (M), Tome IX (op. cit.), p. 278.

34. Tocqueville to Beaumont, June 17, 1858, *Oeuvres* (M), Tome VIII (op. cit.), vol. 3, p. 577.

35. Tocqueville to Bouchitté, Jan. 8, 1858, *Oeuvres* (B), VII, p. 476.

36. *Ibid.*

37. *De la démocratie en Amérique*, vol. 2, p. 30.

38. This is the letter in which Tocqueville described to Mme. Swetchine the anguish of his initial loss of religious certitude in 1820 and his continued "maladie" of doubt. Beaumont did not write that he opposed publication of the letter because it would "establish" that Tocqueville died "pleine de foi," as has been suggested. (See John Lukacs, "The Last Days of Alexis de Tocqueville," *Catholic Historical Review*, L, no. 2 (July 1964), p. 159, note.) What Beaumont wrote was that the letter would cause unpleasant notoriety, which could be averted only if "en même temps qu'on publierait la lettre, d'établir que Tocqueville, que tant de doutes avaient torturé pendant sa vie, est mort plein de foi, et c'est ce qu'il ne nous est pas permis de dire." (Beaumont to Falloux, cited in Redier, op. cit., p. 285.) Beaumont obviously feared that since the letter revealed Tocqueville's religious doubts it would create a "succès de scandale," given the somewhat sanctimonious religious atmosphere of the Second Empire.

One of Falloux's letters to Beaumont on this subject, partially cited by Redier (op. cit., p. 286), has recently been added to the Yale Tocqueville Collection. It suggests that Falloux understood Beaumont's reasons for suppressing the letter, regretted the suppression, and hoped that the letter might be published in the future. Certainly there is no intimation that Falloux regarded Beaumont as an unscrupulous villain wantonly destroying Tocqueville's private papers. See Falloux to Beaumont, June 28, 1865, Y.T. Mss., D.IV.m.

39. André Jardin, "Introduction," *Oeuvres* (M), Tome VIII (op. cit.), vol. 1, p. 42.

40. Beaumont, "Notice sur Alexis de Tocqueville," *Oeuvres* (B), V, p. 120; Ampère, "Appendice", *Oeuvres* (M), Tome XI (op. cit.), p. 453; Redier, op. cit., pp. 294–297.

41. For a summary of the controversy about the meaning of Tocqueville's last religious acts see Doris S. Goldstein, "The Religious Beliefs of Alexis de Tocqueville," *French Historical Studies*, I, no. 4 (Fall 1960), pp. 388–391; also Lukacs, op. cit., pp. 155–170.

42. Louis Baunard, *La foi et ses victoires dans le siècle présent* (Paris, 1884), II, pp. 327–331; Redier, op. cit., pp. 281–299; Lukacs, op. cit., pp. 155–170.

43. Jack Lively, *The Social and Political Thought of Alexis de Tocqueville*

(London, 1962), pp. 183–184; Marvin Zetterbaum, *Tocqueville and the Problem of Democracy* (Stanford, 1967), pp. 118–119; Michael D. Biddiss, "Prophecy and Pragmatism: Gobineau's Confrontation with Tocqueville," *The Historical Journal,* XIII, no. 4 (1970), p. 616.

44. Robert Shackleton, *Montesquieu* (London, 1961), pp. 349–354.

45. Y. T. Mss, C. Vj, Paquet No. 2, Cahier 1, pp. 32, 59.

46. Even Baunard, despite his contention that Tocqueville returned to Catholicism during the last years of his life, recognized that he judged all of the various Christian confessions equally. (See Baunard, op. cit., pp. 248–250.)

47. Sainte-Beuve, op. cit., pp. 293–294.

48. Tocqueville to Gobineau, Oct. 2, 1843, *Oeuvres* (M), Tome IX (op. cit.), p. 57.

49. Tocqueville to Gobineau, Jan. 24, 1857, *Oeuvres* (M), Tome IX (op. cit.), p. 278.

50. Ibid., p. 276.

51. This point has recently been spelled out, in the course of an analysis of the affinities between the thought of Pascal and that of Tocqueville. (See Luis Diez del Corral, *La Mentalidad Politica de Tocqueville con especial referencia a Pascal* [Madrid, 1965], pp. 116–123.)

Chapter II

Religion in America:
The Success of an Experiment

The end of the Restoration and the advent of the July Monarchy forced Tocqueville to take stock of his old loyalties and new political sympathies. While opposed to the Ordinances that sparked the Revolution, he had not desired the fall of the Bourbon dynasty. The new regime could not arouse his enthusiasm, but he thought that the safety and stability of France required its maintenance. He was therefore able to take the oath of allegiance to the new government, which was required of all magistrates, with a clear conscience, if not without agony. Family and childhood friends considered this act as a betrayal of fidelity to the legitimate dynasty. And the government itself was inclined to doubt the loyalty of a son of Hervé de Tocqueville, peer of France and préfect of Charles X.[1]

It was in this painful situation that Tocqueville and Beaumont (who shared the same difficulties) hit upon the idea of studying prison reform in America. Here was a means of temporarily removing themselves from an equivocal position, and possibly they might even further their own careers. From the first, both young men saw their visit in far broader terms than those defined in their official mission, which was simply to investigate American prison systems. Their aim was nothing less than studying "the mirage in the West," its society, its people, its government. What was the origin of this interest? The work of René Rémond, by revealing the sources of French interest in the United States during the Restoration, has made it possible to put Tocqueville and Beaumont's decision to visit America into a larger perspective. Much of this interest was politically motivated, with American institutions becoming yet another weapon in the arsenal of political liberals, and even of a section of the right.[2] Evidently, the two young men wished to see and judge for themselves.

From May 1831, until February 1832, Tocqueville and Beaumont travelled about the United States and Canada, and throughout their sojourn Tocqueville remained fascinated by American religious life. He was enormously curious about the religious beliefs of the people of the United States and of Canada, and about the interplay of religion with other American institutions. His interest in this aspect of American life owed much, as Pierson has noted, to that "burning concern" with religious questions kindled by personal doubts and difficulties.[3] In addition, the role played by religion in Restoration politics, and especially in the events leading to the July Revolution, had not escaped his notice. Here was an opportunity for the nascent social analyst to explore the different religious situations of France and America. Comparison was of the essence, and Tocqueville's travel notes attest to his remarkable ability to frame questions and elicit replies on the basis of which meaningful comparisons could be made. A recent essay has pointed out how he was aided in this task by his use of categories supplied by Montesquieu's theory.[4] Using these categories, he then relied heavily upon the data gathered in America, as is demonstrated by examining the raw materials from which *De la démocratie en Amérique* was fashioned. His conclusions were to become the basis for broader generalizations concerning the role of religion in modern society, but it was the American experience that served as his point of departure and remained as his guide.

Having remarked less than a week after his arrival in the United States that the Americans "appear on the whole a religious people," Tocqueville thereafter took every opportunity to discover whether his first impression had been valid. Again and again, he questioned Catholic and Protestant, Northerner and Southerner, merchant and lawyer. The replies, together with his own observations, admitted of only one conclusion: irreligion was not to be found, and Christianity was immeasurably more vigorous in America than in France.[5] The strict observance of the Sabbath especially caught his attention, leading him to comment that "these republicans scarcely resemble our French liberals."[6] Tocqueville was gratified to learn that republicanism need not mean irreligion, but he was also puzzled by the Americans' manner of belief. They did not find it necessary to argue, to prove the validity of Christian doctrine, but simply accepted Christianity without discussion.[7] This was particularly astonishing given the multiplicity of sects. How could Christianity be respected, let alone believed, when each sect fervently held to doctrines rejected by the others?[8]

That a Frenchman should find this situation baffling is readily understandable. French opinion during the Restoration was not inclined to attribute much importance to the role of religion in American life precisely because of these apparent anomalies.[9] In the effort to solve the enigma Tocqueville repeatedly asked his American informants whether religious indifference and scepticism might not lie behind the solid facade of Christianity. His interlocutors insisted that most Americans truly believed: they set forth in terrifying detail the disastrous social consequences suffered by those known to be unbelievers.[10] From these accounts and from his own observations, Tocqueville drew the conclusions that he was to present in *De la démocratie en Amérique:* Christianity was ubiquitous and beyond discussion in America, but in terms of content it tended to stress morality rather than dogma. Accordingly, the great number of sects did not weaken religion, since all adhered to the basic principles of Christianity. Although they might disagree with each other privately, they all "preach the same moral law in the name of God."[11] Tocqueville considered the American concern with morality instead of dogma to be both cause and effect. It was the effect of the proliferation of sects that resulted in emphasis on commonly held moral principles rather than on doctrinal differences. But the very emphasis on morality caused the dilution of doctrinal substance, which led Americans to lose sight of the "otherworldly" essence of religion.[12]

And what of Catholicism? It was with special interest that Tocqueville sought to determine how the Church had been affected by its introduction into a democratic society. Almost immediately upon arriving in the United States, he noted that Catholicism seemed to be increasing in importance at the very time that it was under attack in Europe.[13] His informants stated that immigration was partially the reason, but that there were also many conversions.[14] The rapidity with which he arrived at an explanation for the large number of conversions may have been due to previous knowledge of Catholic missionary activities in the United States.[15] At any rate, after only six weeks in the United States Tocqueville explained the matter to his friend, Kergolay. Catholicism, he wrote, was becoming attractive to many Americans who felt the need for religion and to whom the looseness of Protestantism had become a burden. In addition, Catholicism appealed to members of the working classes, because it "seized vividly upon the feelings and the mind."[16] The same points are reiterated in the *Démocratie,* where they are adduced as evidence that Catholicism, because of its unity and uniformity, was suited to democratic societies.[17] This generalization was

17

important to Tocqueville's larger didactic purpose. Probably for this reason he centered his short discussion of the progress of Catholicism in the United States upon conversion, instead of upon the more obvious and significant factor of immigration.

Increase in Church membership was only one indication of the strong and secure position enjoyed by Catholicism in America. Tocqueville described with satisfaction the élan and enthusiasm of the Catholic priesthood in the United States and Canada, and the ability of the Church to live honored and respected by those outside as well as within its own communion.[18] His explanation of these gratifying phenomena is well-known: Catholicism, in common with all other religions in the United States, has been willing to accept separation of church and state and to adapt to the conditions of a democratic society. But how was it that American Catholics thought so differently from their counterparts in Europe? Tocqueville observed, for example, that in both Canada and the United States it was the Catholics who held the most democratic opinions. At first he attributed this, not to the inherent tendencies of the religion, but to the fact that "these Catholics are poor and almost all of them come from a country where the aristocracy is Protestant."[19] The political attitudes of American Catholics followed from their social and economic status: these material interests were strong enough to sever the natural links between a religious doctrine and its political consequences.

In the *Démocratie,* however, Tocqueville proceeded differently. Here he was intent upon proving the compatibility between Catholicism and democracy in theory as well as in practice. He argued that the Catholic tenet of the equality of all men before God was favorable to democratic tendencies. Catholics would, therefore, naturally support political equality, if there is separation of church and state. Only after having made this point did he mention the significance of social position and minority status in determining the political attitudes of American Catholics. And, in a preceding passage, there was the eminently reasonable remark that if the Catholics are not led by their beliefs to democratic convictions, neither are they necessarily opposed to them.[20]

What is the reader to make of this murky reasoning? Is Tocqueville arguing that there is an inherent compatibility between certain aspects of Catholicism and democracy? Or is he saying that there is no necessary opposition between the two, as shown by the American experience? The difficulty is that in the *Démocratie* Tocqueville does not wish to confine himself to the latter position. To point out that in America the inferior social position and minority status of most Catholics insured their democratic tendencies was of no relevance to France, a primarily Catholic nation. Hence he stressed, although not without inconsistency, that Catholic doctrine itself contained ideas favorable to democracy. To some extent these pages of the *Démocratie* show Tocqueville's predilection for searching out generalized theoretical explanations of his empirical findings, but in this case, it is surely his didactic intent that is uppermost. Whether in the *Démocratie*, in *L'Ancien Régime et la Révolution*, or in his political career, he was always to insist upon the compatibility of Catholicism and democracy.

From his letters and diaries one does not get the impression that Tocqueville was especially curious about the beliefs or organizational structures of the Protestant churches. Coming from a Catholic background, what naturally caught his attention was the lack of emphasis upon dogma. His image of American Protestantism was one of constantly proliferating sects. As they separated themselves from the older branches, they moved further and further away from the parent faith, Catholicism. The end result of this process, he feared, would be the destruction of Christianity. Perhaps it was for this reason, because he believed that Protestantism was a halfway house destined to disappear before Catholicism or the onslaughts of "reason," that he paid so little attention to the teachings of the various Protestant sects.[21] He was sufficiently curious about Unitarianism to attend a Sunday service and to question John Quincy Adams and William Ellery Channing himself about the sect. Although he wavered between describing Unitarianism as pure deism or as the last frail outpost separating Christianity from natural religion, his evaluation was nevertheless acute. Unitarianism appealed to the prosperous and educated classes, to those willing to carry Protestantism to its logical conclusion and embrace a religion of reason.[22] He appeared to regard the sect with a mixture of fear and fascination, possibly because of the manner in which it dealt with religious problems, which Tocqueville found disturbing.

But if a certain dryness, as well as emphasis upon reason and morality, were characteristic of Unitarianism, these terms were far from an adequate description of American Protestantism during the Jacksonian period. At the very time Tocqueville was in America the Protestant sects were experiencing that outburst of revivalism that has come to be called the Second Great Awakening. And yet he showed little awareness of its nature or significance. He was told that in the West and South, where Methodism was most influential, the quality of religious life differed from that in the

North. In the West religion was "less enlightened", but religious feeling itself was perhaps more profound than in any other area, including New England.[23] He utilized this information in a chapter of the *Démocratie* entitled, "Why Some Americans Manifest a Sort of Fanatical Spiritualism." In tone and content, as well as in title, these pages reflected a somewhat contemptuous attitude towards the revival movement. The purpose of the chapter was to illustrate how the prevailing concern for material well-being among Americans gave rise to a wild and unrestrained religiosity. Since a taste for the infinite and immortal is rooted in human nature, the stifling of these instincts because of exclusive concern with material welfare, breeds the reaction of an excessive spiritualism. This passage is a typical example of how Tocqueville's assumptions about human nature became the basis for sociological generalizations. It is, however, singularly insensitive about the revival movement itself. The latter was used merely to make the point that in America one extreme breeds the other extreme of "religious insanity."[24] In short, revivalism, which has been described as the "most striking characteristic" of American religion in the nineteenth century, was dismissed by Tocqueville as an aberrant and atypical phenomenon.[25]

The result is that his description of American Protestantism has a flatness, a one-dimensional quality. There is, for example, no consideration of the connections between membership in the various sects and social class, nor awareness that the fervent idealism produced by evangelical religion spawned many reform movements in nineteenth-century America. Admittedly, Tocqueville did not intend to study religion in America in any exhaustive fashion; nevertheless, it is surprising that his interest in the interplay of religion, society, and politics did not lead to a deeper and fuller analysis. The explanation is probably that his personality and background gave him little sympathy or understanding for the doctrines and attitudes of the Second Great Awakening. And his own prejudices were reinforced by the views of his informants, many of whom spoke condescendingly about the revival movement. But Tocqueville's failure to appreciate the richness and diversity of Ameican Protestantism raises larger questions, directly related to his statements about the quality of American religious life. Had he examined more closely the ideas and influence of Methodism, Baptism, and evangelical Presbyterianism, he might not have come away with the impression that American Protestantism was merely a dry moralism, devoid of real feeling and substance. And yet it is precisely this judgment, always implicit and sometimes explicit in the *Démocratie,* that has been accepted by many historians and sociologists as valid and perceptive.[26]

While Tocqueville was more-or-less indifferent to the internal beliefs and practices of the sects, his attention was caught by the effects of Protestantism upon American political life.[27] Indeed, his interlocutors made it difficult for him to ignore this subject, since they informed him frequently that Protestantism was inseparable from the republican and democratic institutions of the United States.[28] The journal entry in which he attempted to come to grips with the question of the compatibility between Catholicism and democracy was an indication of how deeply he had been struck by the insistence of his informants that Protestantism, democracy, and republicanism were indissolubly linked.[29] In the *Démocratie* he explicitly acknowledged the affinity between Protestantism, "a democratic and republican religion." and American political ideas and practices.[30] It was to New England Puritanism, rather than to Protestantism in general, that Tocqueville traced the origins of the American democratic ethos.[31] His description of the colonization of New England was truly in the tradition of what Wesley Frank Craven has called "the legend of the founding fathers."[32] Tocqueville emphasized the Puritan union of religious ardor with devotion to liberty, and concluded that the civilization that emerged from this alliance "has been like a beacon lit upon a hill," influencing all of America.[33] In New England personal rights and self-government first became accepted principles of government and legislation, as a result of the republican and democratic affinities of Puritanism itself. Tocqueville did not explain how these political views emerged out of Puritan theology. The strength of his analysis was in its perception that "the nonconformist conscience" was able to combine acceptance of authority in one area with a taste for independence and innovation in politics. He made no secret of his admiration for the Puritan amalgam of the "spirit of religion and the spirit of liberty," and for its effects upon American development.[34] Because of this fortunate heritage, the United States became a society in which religion and liberty, far from being hostile to each other, were staunch allies. This, for Tocqueville, was the proper state of affairs and one that he hoped that France could emulate.

But how could Protestant America provide an appropriate model for Catholic France? Admitting that there were natural affinities between Protestantism, liberty, and democracy, Tocqueville argued that, under certain conditions, Catholicism could accommodate itself to new political ideas and institutions. The most important of these conditions, as every reader of the *Démocratie* knows, is separation of church and state. Indeed,

21

the role that Tocqueville assigned to separation in his treatment of religion in America is of such paramount importance that it sometimes takes on the appearance of a *deus ex machina*. Not only did he maintain that separation could make Catholicism safe for democracy (to paraphrase Seymour Drescher), but he also insisted that this was the most important single factor accounting for the strength of religion in America. As a result, the Puritan influence becomes only one component—and not necessarily the crucial one—in explaining that symbiosis of religion and liberty achieved by the United States. Undeniably, his estimate of the importance of separation rested in large part upon his own observations and upon the evidence supplied by informants. Both Catholic priests and Protestant clergymen, as well as laymen of all religious persuasions, affirmed that all of the denominations benefited from the American separation of spiritual and temporal power.[35] Tocqueville accepted these statements and, in the *Démocratie,* fashioned them into a cogent and forceful argument.

He did not arrive in the United States devoid of opinions concerning the proper relationship between religion and politics. Dislike of the policies of Charles X, together with his incipient liberal sympathies, led him to question the French pattern of church–state relations. A few months before the outbreak of the July Revolution he expressed the conviction that the close ties between religion and politics that existed in France were detrimental to Catholicism itself, and therefore should be broken.[36] Although this remark need not be interpreted as outright advocacy of separation of church and state, it does reflect a dissatisfaction with the French religious situation that was widespread during the last years of the Restoration. In 1825, in response to the enactment of legislation penalizing sacrilege as a civil crime, the possibility of disestablishment emerged from the domain of closet philosophy and was openly discussed in the Chamber of Deputies and in the press. It was, in fact, the *Société de la morale chrétienne,* to which Tocqueville belonged, that most explicitly espoused both religious liberty and separation of church and state.[37] And by the late 1820s that segment of the right led by Chateaubriand was also praising religious freedom as it existed in America.[38]

Allusions to America were frequent among those who disapproved of the role played by religion in Restoration politics. These critics pointed to the American discovery that the independence of the spiritual from the temporal power was not only practicable, but resulted in the strengthening of religion itself. Support for this view was to be found among some French priests, whose personal experience had taught them that Catholicism in

22

America benefited from freedom of religion and separation of church and state.[39] One of the most distinguished among these ecclesiastics was Mgr. de Cheverus, who had held the diocese of Boston until his return to France in 1823. According to Jardin, Mgr. de Cheverus was a close friend of the Tocqueville family, and was probably among those from whom Tocqueville gained an interest in American ideas and institutions.[40] It is quite likely that before his departure for America, the latter had heard sympathetic descriptions of American church–state relationships from a highly respected and knowledgeable source. In any case, there is little doubt that Tocqueville came to America not altogether unprepared for what he was to find, and favorably disposed toward alternatives to the French system of church–state arrangements.

His own observations and the opinions of his American informants transformed sympathy into conviction, so that Tocqueville's self-imposed task in the *Démocratie* was one of explaining to his compatriots, and perhaps to himself, why disestablishment strengthened religion. His argument was based upon the premise that religion is natural to human beings: "Unbelief is an accident, and faith is the only permanent state of mankind."[41] Although clearly reflecting personal beliefs and assumptions, for Tocqueville this was also a psychological generalization about human nature. It followed that religion, if left to itself, will always be able to maintain its hold, since it derived its strength from fundamental human needs and aspirations. Connections with the temporal power—any temporal power—are therefore unnecessary. Although they may, for a time, give religion an increased influence, this is bought at the price of exposure to the passions and hostilities of the political arena. What is more, governments are themselves more or less ephemeral, and a religion that is not independent risks the destruction that must inevitably overtake its temporal protector. It is particularly dangerous for religion to tie itself to the fortunes of government in an age of democratization, Tocqueville warned, since change and agitation characterize democratic societies. If a religion is forced to take part in these political struggles because of its connection with the state, it will become subject to similar ferment. The clergy in the United States realized this danger, and in order to preserve their spiritual influence, the sects renounced all ties with the state. By thus voluntarily restricting the sphere of its activities, religion remains strong and secure in America, despite capricious political conditions.[42]

Tocqueville's explanation of how separation came about in the United States constitutes a kind of logical coda to his argument, and is, in fact, interesting for just this reason. Disestablishment is presented as the consequence of a deliberate sociological judgment on the part of the American clergy, rather than as the result of specific historical events and developments. In terms of Tocqueville's didactic aims it was pointless, and possibly prejudicial, to describe to his French audience the weakness of religious establishments in the colonies before the American Revolution, the alliance between rationalists and pietists that brought about separation, or the initial fears that disestablishment might lead to infidelity.[43] And so he omits consideration of the complex chain of circumstances that ended in disestablishment, and offers instead an explanation that did have relevance for France: Americans regard religion as a bulwark of their society, and to protect it from the effects of political and social instability, they have separated church and state. In effect, he is saying that as the tide of democratization inevitably rises in France, the Church should beware of the danger of being tied to the temporal power. Instead, it should endeavor to emulate the American example.

These pages of the *Démocratie* are far more than exposition. They are an eloquent plea for separation of church and state in France. Tocqueville wished to convince his French readers that hostility between liberty and religion is unnatural: it existed in France because the Church became involved in the struggles of an outmoded political structure against new ideas. The solution then, would be to destroy these ties, and religion will regain its natural dominion. Although there is no doubt about his sincerity in prescribing this remedy for French religio-political conflicts, there are ambiguities. For example, his argument centers on demonstrating that separation strengthens, rather than weakens, the hold of religion. Nowhere in the *Démocratie,* or in any of his other writings, did Tocqueville assert that the liberal concept of a state unconcerned with the religious commitments of its citizens demands separation. Did he assume that disestablishment was the logical corollary to freedom of religion? Was his emphasis on the benefits that would accrue to religion merely a means of making his objective more palatable to the French? Or did he see separation, not as a principle, but merely as a device that could strengthen religion? Other difficulties converge about the question of the extent to which Tocqueville actually thought of the American pattern of church–state relationships as a practical model for France. Some answers to these questions will emerge from subsequent examination of his response to French church–state problems.

Just as all religions in America have been willing to accept the separation of spiritual from temporal power, so too they have accommodated themselves in other respects to democratic conditions. Tocqueville's account of these adjustments is again distinctly hortatory in tone, and directed at teaching the French how religion can be preserved and strengthened. The clergy of all denominations in the United States, recognizing that public opinion is all-powerful in a democracy, has been wise enough to conform to the popular will in all but the essentials of faith. For example, "democratic man" is impatient of forms, rituals, external observances; and this emphasis on the spirit rather than on the forms of religious worship has not been opposed. Tocqueville makes a point of adding that the Catholic clergy has also concluded that ritual and observance must be limited. Except in spiritual matters, the members of a democratic society will not accept the principle of authority, and they will not tolerate attempts by the clergy to induce men to abandon the pursuit of material well-being. Hence, in the United States no religion alienates the majority by attempting to exercise authority in nonreligious matters. Asceticism is not preached, but the ministers of all the sects try to regulate and restrain the desire for wealth. It is this kind of flexibility that has gained the support of public opinion for all the denominations, and has resulted in the strength and ubiquity of religion in America.[44]

For those who are acquainted with the work of the consensus school of American history these remarks will have a familiar ring. And with reason, since Tocqueville has become the mentor of those historians and sociologists who stress the existence of a distinctive and commonly accepted American ideology. His description of religion in the United States as pervasive and yet doctrinally dilute, together with his awareness of how republicanism, patriotism, and religion have blended into "the American way of life," are considered by Bellah, Boorstin, and Lipset to be valid and perceptive. According to these scholars, Tocqueville perceived that religion, defined in a broad, nondenominational sense, formed the matrix of the American value system, and thereby served as a highly successful means of social integration.[45] In striking contrast to this appraisal is Perry Miller's judgment that Tocqueville's "pages on religion in *De la Démocratie en Amérique* are probably the least perceptive he ever wrote.[46] While agreeing with Tocqueville's description of the ubiquity of religion in America, Miller criticizes his readiness to assume that American Protestantism lacked depth and feeling. Sectarianism and separation of church and state did not, according to Miller, reduce religion to the lowest common denominator of a dry moralism. Instead, the revivalism of the Second Great

Awakening "made religious exultation an adjunct to the national vigor."[47]

Miller's strictures are very much to the point, and illustrate the need for greater wariness in the use of the *Démocratie* as a primary source.[48] John Higham has suggested that the consensus historians "homogenized" American history, and in the same fashion Tocqueville homogenized American religion. Because his aim was to show how religion acted as the guardian of American values and stability, he neglected the fact that the very vitality and idealism of the sects could—and did—engender social conflict as well as social integration. But although he exaggerated the extent to which religion in the United States was merely morality and ideology, church historians, too, have stressed the tendency of American Protestantism to become a "culture religion."[49] Nor was Tocqueville unaware that the conversion of religion into religiosity exacted a heavy price. Although deeply impressed by the pervasiveness of Christianity in America, and therefore little inclined to cavil, he did comment upon the hypocrisy that must result when the entire weight of public opinion enforces religious conformity.[50] In a sense, Tocqueville's analysis mirrors his own Janus-like attitude towards religion: reverence for sincere religious feeling and yet emphasis upon the secular utility of religion. The former viewpoint induced scepticism about the quality of American belief, but the latter led to approval of American efforts to foster religion because of its this-worldly benefits.

The dominance of the functional posture in the *Démocratie* is undeniable and understandable, since Tocqueville's purpose is to prove to a French audience that a free and democratic nation cannot exist without religion. The Americans have realized this and strengthened Christianity, so that it acts as a check upon tendencies toward instability emanating from politics and intellectual life.[51] If, however, religion is allowed to become so weak that it cannot fulfill this function, freedom will degenerate into lawlessness and license. To escape from anarchy men will become willing to submit to a despot who can impose order upon society. In short, there were only two practical alternatives for "democratic man": "if faith be wanting in him, he must be subject; and if he be free, he must believe."[52]

This dictum was to remain the cornerstone of Tocqueville's political faith. But it was not a dictum that could inspire a devoted French citizen and patriot with a sense of security about his own country, where the advocates of liberty and of religion commonly regarded each other as foes. And so in the *Démocratie* Tocqueville endeavored to prove that this mutual enmity was not inevitable, but rather the result of adventitious circum-

26

stances. If ties between church and state were broken, if the partisans of liberty and the partisans of religion could be made to realize that their strife was unnatural and destructive, then France could face the democratic future more hopefully.[53] It was the American experience that gave Tocqueville not merely hope, but proof that democratization need not result in the weakening of religion. In the United States both Catholicism and Protestantism had successfully passed the test imposed by new political and social conditions. Could Christianity in France replicate this achievement? The answer given in the *Démocratie* was a cautious affirmative, but the question would continue to preoccupy Tocqueville's thought and his active political life.

Notes

1. For the biographical material in this paragraph and the next see Pierson, op. cit., ch. II; Tocqueville to Kergolay, Aug. 17, 1830, Y. T. Mss, A.VII; Tocqueville to Hippolyte de Tocqueville, Aug. 18, 1830, *Oeuvres* (B), VI, pp. 6–8.
2. René Rémond, *Les Etats-Unis devant l'opinion française, 1815-1852* (Paris, 1962), vol. 2, pp. 449-651.
3. Pierson, op. cit., p. 151.
4. Melvin Richter, "The Uses of Theory: Tocqueville's Adaptation of Montesquieu," in Melvin Richter (ed.), *Essays in Theory and History* (Cambridge, Mass., 1970), p. 87.
5. Tocqueville, *Oeuvres* (M), Tome V (*Voyages en Sicile et aux Etats-Unis*), pp. 77, 107, 113-117, 231, 293; Y. T. Mss, C.Vj, Paquet No. 2, Cahier 1, p. 61; Tocqueville to Kergolay, June 29, 1831, *Oeuvres* (B), V, pp. 312, 314. The reader will note how Tocqueville identifies "religion" with "Christianity," the latter defined broadly to include both Catholicism and all varieties of Protestantism.
6. Tocqueville to Eugène Stoffels, July 28, 1831, *Oeuvres* (B), V, p. 418.
7. Y. T. Mss, C.Vj, Paquet No. 2, Cahier 1, pp. 59-60, 64; see also *De la démocratie en Amérique*, vol. 2, p. 14.
8. Tocqueville, *Oeuvres* (M), Tome V (op. cit.), p. 293; *De la démocratie en Amérique*, vol. 1, p. 304, vol. 2, p. 14.
9. Rémond, op. cit., pp. 742-743.
10. Tocqueville, *Oeuvres* (M), Tome V (op. cit.), pp. 107, 114-115.
11. *De la démocratie en Amérique*, vol. 1, p. 304.
12. Ibid., pp. 304-307.
13. Tocqueville to Comtesse de Tocqueville, May 15, 1831, *Oeuvres* (B), VII, p. 13; Tocqueville to Kergolay, June 29, 1831, *Oeuvres* (B), V, pp. 312-313.
14. Tocqueville, *Oeuvres* (M), Tome V (op. cit.), pp. 72, 74, 116-117, 230.
15. Rémond has shown that the French were very much interested in this subject. (Rémond, op. cit., vol. 1, ch. 3, esp. pp. 145-154.)
16. Tocqueville to Kergolay, June 29, 1831, *Oeuvres* (B), V, pp. 312-313.
17. *De la démocratie en Amérique*, vol. 2, pp. 35-36.

18. Tocqueville, *Oeuvres* (M), Tome V (op. cit.), pp. 72-74, 77-79, 82, 113, 116-117.

19. Ibid., p. 179.

20. *De la démocratie en Amérique,* vol. 1, pp. 301-303.

21. Tocqueville to Kergolay, June 29, 1831, *Oeuvres* (B), V, pp. 313-314; Tocqueville, *Oeuvres* (M), Tome V (op. cit.), pp. 154-155; *De la démocratie en Amérique,* vol. 2, pp. 35-36.

22. Tocqueville to Kergolay, June 29, 1831, *Oeuvres* (B), V, pp. 313-314; Tocqueville, *Oeuvres* (M), Tome V (op. cit.), pp. 99-101.

23. Tocqueville, *Oeuvres* (M), Tome V (op. cit.), pp. 130-131, 142.

24. *De la démocratie en Amérique,* vol. 2, pp. 140-141.

25. See A. Leland Jamison, "Religions on the Christian Perimeter," in James Ward Smith and A. Leland Jamison, *The Shaping of American Religion* (Princeton, 1961), p. 194. Sydney E. Ahlstrom, in *A Religious History of the American People* (New Haven, 1972), chaps. 26-28, provides a good account of nineteenth-century American revivalism and its effects. Tocqueville considered deleting the chapter itself from the *Démocratie,* surely an indication that he regarded the subject-matter as more-or-less inconsequential.

26. *De la démocratie en Amérique,* vol. 1, pp. 304-307, vol. 2, pp. 33-34, 132-133. See pp. 25-26, for a discussion of the influence exercised by Tocqueville's assessments.

27. Schleifer (op. cit., pp. 13-16) has pointed out that Tocqueville's original "grand design" for the *Démocratie* envisaged a tripartite organization, comprising "political society," "civil society," and "religious society." I would suggest that Tocqueville abandoned the idea of a separate section dealing with "religious society" because, aside perhaps from Catholicism, he was interested in religion in America primarily in terms of its political ramifications. Hence, as Schleifer notes, the task of describing the sects was turned over to Beaumont, who paid some attention to the subject in the text and in an appendix of *Marie, ou l'esclavage aux Etats-Unis* (Paris, 1835).

28. Tocqueville, *Oeuvres* (M), Tome V (op. cit.), pp. 96-97, 102, 207.

29. Ibid., p. 179.

30. *De la démocratie en Amérique,* vol. 1, p. 301.

31. This point has been made by Pierson, op. cit., p. 757, note.

32. Wesley Frank Craven, *The Legend of the Founding Fathers* (New York, 1956). See esp. ch. 1.

33. *De la démocratie en Amérique,* vol. 1, p. 30.

34. Ibid., pp. 42-43.

35. Tocqueville, *Oeuvres* (M), Tome V (op. cit.), pp. 138, 165, 230-232.

36. Tocqueville to Charles Stoffels, Apr. 21, 1830, Y. T. Mss, A.VII.

37. For an account of the controversy aroused by the sacrilege bill, and the role of the Société in opposing it, see Mary S. Hartman, "The Sacrilege Law of 1825 in France: A Study in Anticlericalism and Mythmaking," *Journal of Modern History,* 44, no. 1 (March 1972), p. 35, and Georges Weill, *Histoire de l'idée laïque en France au XIXe siècle* (Paris, 1929), pp. 20-22, 48-55.

38. Rémond, op. cit., vol. 2, pp. 644-645.

39. Ibid., vol. 1, pp. 158-160, vol. 2, pp. 549-552, 643-644.

40. André Jardin, "Introduction," *Oeuvres* (M), Tome VIII (op. cit.), vol. 1, p. 18.

41. *De la démocratie en Amérique,* vol. 1, p. 310.

42. Ibid., pp. 308-315 for the material in this paragraph.

43. See Winthrop S. Hudson, *American Protestantism* (Chicago, 1961), pp. 49-78, and Sidney Mead, *The Lively Experiment* (New York, 1963), pp. 38-71.

44. *De la démocratie en Amérique,* vol. 2, pp. 29-34.

45. See Robert N. Bellah, "Civil Religion in America," *Daedalus* (Winter 1967), pp. 1-21; Daniel J. Boorstin, *The Genius of American Politics* (Chicago, 1958), pp. 133-160; Seymour M. Lipset, *The First New Nation* (New York, 1963), pp. 140-169. On the more general use of Tocqueville by consensus historians see John Higham, "The Cult of the 'American Consensus': Homogenizing Our History," *Commentary,* XXVII (Feb. 1959), pp. 93-100.

46. Perry Miller, "From the Covenant to the Revival," in Smith and Jamison, op. cit., p. 365.

47. Ibid., p. 362.

48. This point is made in Lynn L. Marshall and Seymour Drescher, "American Historians and Tocqueville's *Democracy,"Journal of American History,* LV, no. 3 (Dec. 1968), pp. 512-532.

49. Ahlstrom, op. cit., ch. 50; Hudson, op. cit., pp. 109-111, 135; H. Richard Niebuhr, "The Protestant Movement and Democracy in the United States," in Smith and Jamison, op, cit., pp. 20-71.

50. *De la démocratie en Amérique,* vol. 1, p. 304.

51. Ibid., pp. 305-306.

52. Ibid., vol. 2, p. 29.

53. Ibid., vol. 1, pp. 308, 314.

Chapter III

The Church and the July Monarchy:
The Effort at Reconciliation

The success of the first part of the *Démocratie,* published in 1835, gave Tocqueville recognition and new, influential connections. Prized as they were in themselves, these rewards of authorship were also a means of furthering his desire for a political career. To follow the example of his great ancestor, Malesherbes, and play a prominent part in the affairs of his country was, for Tocqueville, both a matter of personal ambition and of obligation. His taste for fame and power was harnessed to an intense belief that it was his duty to use the political arena, as well as the pen, to help France achieve a stable and free society. In the midst of writing the second part of the *Démocratie,* much of his attention was focused on obtaining a seat in the Chamber of Deputies, an ambition that was fulfilled in 1839, a year before the appearance of the book. Thereafter, and until 1851, when he retired from public life because of opposition to the government of Louis Napoleon, he served in both the local and national legislative bodies of the July Monarchy and the Second Republic.

Tocqueville stated that his principal aim in entering politics was to foster the reconciliation of "the liberal spirit and the spirit of religion."[1] This remark should be understood in terms of his conviction that France could not become a free and stable society until the estrangement between French Catholics and the revolutionary ideals of 1789 had ceased to exist.[2] But what kind of political action did he contemplate in pursuit of his goal? What obstacles might political action overcome? How might a statesman help to insure that the Catholic faith in France successfully met the

31

challenge of new conditions? To say that Tocqueville's answers to these questions reflected his appraisal of the religious situation during the July Monarchy would appear to be no more than a truism. And yet this appraisal, in itself idiosyncratic, must be examined with some care.

Just as the *Démocratie* intimates, it was in church–state relations that Tocqueville found the key to past and present discontents. He explained that during the reign of Louis XIV, the Church became subservient to the state and gradually took on the aspect of a political rather than a religious institution. Between 1715 and 1789 religious belief weakened until Catholicism finally lost its hold over men's minds while its clergy became rich and privileged.[3] In its misguided effort to return to the pre-Revolutionary pattern of church–state relationships, the Restoration brought about renewed hostility to Catholicism. Because of the political influence of the clergy, irreligion became a form of opposition to the regime. The July Revolution broke the ties binding church and state, and the tide of anti-Catholicism was stemmed. A tendency back to religion can now be distinguished, especially among the students. They are becoming convinced of the necessity of faith and either do believe or would like to believe. This is attested by the remarkable success of the Abbé Lacordaire's public sermons.*[4]

What is striking in this appraisal is the extent to which Tocqueville regarded church–state relationships as determining French attitudes towards Catholicism. There is no doubt that the efforts made by Charles X to renew the alliance between throne and altar bred hostility to the Church and led to the anticlerical outbursts that followed the Revolution of 1830. And once the Church no longer enjoyed the active support of the government, it began to gain public sympathy and esteem, so that by 1835 there was evidence of a Catholic revival. But the causes of this revival were many and diverse and cannot be attributed solely to the neutrality of the July Monarchy with respect to the Church. Government neutrality itself was at best only relative, as Tocqueville was to point out ten years later.[5] From 1833 until the demise of the July Monarchy, all ministries were sympathetic to the Church, in the hope of weaning it from Legitimism and using it against the Left. The bourgeoisie had become frightened by the *émeutes* of the early years of the regime and began to think that it would be

---

*Tocqueville was referring to the sermons that Lacordaire, an eloquent orator as well as a liberal Catholic priest, delivered at Notre-Dame in March 1835. See Philip Spencer, *Politics of Belief in Nineteenth-Century France* (New York, 1954), ch. 5, for a brief description of the excitement caused by these sermons.

wise to promote religion, at least among the workers. Then there was the entire cluster of intellectual influences: the Christian aspirations of the Romantics; the well-publicized religious regrets of liberals like Jouffroy; the vague social Christianity of Buchez; and the respect for Catholic hierarchy on the part of the Saint-Simonians.[6] The point is not that Tocqueville's judgment was wrong; without question, the end of Bourbon clericalism was the precondition of Catholic revival in France. It is rather that throughout the July Monarchy he persisted in regarding the separation of the Church from politics as a kind of talisman which, in itself, accounted for a complex set of phenomena. Because he began with the premise that religious belief was "natural," it followed that hostility to Catholicism was an "unnatural" phenomenon attributable to defective church–state relationships.

Ironically, for all of his repeated adjurations and admonitions, it is not clear what Tocqueville envisioned as the proper pattern of relations between church and state in France. To the reader of the *Démocratie* it seems obvious that he wished France to emulate the American model of disestablishment, of churches as voluntary organizations. In the context of French society this meant the end of the Napoleonic Concordat, a measure that Tocqueville neither advocated publicly nor even discussed in his private correspondence. His relatively sanguine assessment of the position of Catholicism during the 1830s was, in fact, based upon the assumption that separation between the spiritual and temporal powers had been achieved by the July Revolution. The evidence suggests, then, that he was prepared to accept something far less drastic than separation in the American sense for his own country. From one point of view this is not surprising, since demands for disestablishment were neither frequent nor vehement during the July Monarchy. With the waning of hostility to Catholicism after 1830, explicit condemnation of the Concordat became rare, especially in the "notable" circles in which Tocqueville moved. It was the union of throne and altar as it had existed during the Restoration that had incurred opprobrium, and the policy of neutrality as practiced by the July Monarchy seemed a satisfactory alternative. Indeed, in the years between 1830 and 1848 the erstwhile Restoration liberals, now part of the governing élite, had no desire to free the Church from state supervision.[7]

But did Tocqueville, who knew and eulogized the American system, share these views? And if so, how should his fervent espousal of separation in the *Démocratie* be construed? To the first question, the answer must be that despite whatever he envisioned as an ideal situation possibly attainable in the future, for the present he was content with the Concordat as the basis of French church–state relations. This is not to deny that his reading of events before 1830, together with his knowledge of Montesquieu, had convinced him that the confounding of the religious and temporal powers was inherently pernicious. Nor is it to deny that he sincerely believed in freedom of religion together with freedom of association and freedom of teaching. However, absolute separation in the American sense need not necessarily follow, as the experience of England indicated. Tocqueville did not consider the English pattern of an established church and freedom of religion to be unsatisfactory, provided that the Anglican Church did not engender hostility by interfering in politics.[8] His approbation of the American system had not been based upon its adherence to the abstract principle of separation, but rather upon its ability to strengthen religion. What is being suggested, then, is that Tocqueville's eulogies of separation of church and state in the *Démocratie* should not be understood as an effort to have the French copy the First Amendment. Rather, it was an attempt to persuade his countrymen to accept the spirit, if not the letter, of American church–state relations. Disestablishment was the means whereby one country, with a particular history and set of circumstances, had been able to assure the continued hold of religion in a democratic society. Other methods might be more practicable in other countries; for France the avoidance of further conflict involving Catholicism was the most urgent necessity. The abrogation of the Concordat, or even discussion of such a measure by responsible men, would raise up the ghosts of quarrels but recently laid and precipitate new strife. Only the most zealous and single-minded advocate of separation could judge the end to be worth the risks: in a word, a Lamennais and not a Tocqueville. For the latter, there was no practical alternative to the existing framework of French church–state arrangements. He was aware that as long as the Concordat existed, the independence of the secular and the ecclesiastical powers was precarious, but he hoped that memory of the débacle of the Restoration would insure tact and neutrality.[9]

Mention of Lamennais raises the question of whether Tocqueville was influenced by the "Avenir" movement, that first gallant attempt from within the Catholic fold to unite the Church to the new society that had emerged from the French Revolution. Tocqueville's emphasis upon the need for religion in modern society, his insistence that Catholicism could be reconciled with liberalism, and his belief that the Church should hold itself aloof from the temporal power, are similar to the ideas put forward by the

34

nascent liberal Catholicism of 1830 and 1831. *L'Avenir* began publication almost six months before Tocqueville and Beaumont left for America in 1831. It is therefore possible that Tocqueville was familiar with the newspaper, or perhaps even with *Des Progrès de la révolution et de la guerre contre l'Eglise*, published by Lamennais in 1829 and immensely influential.[10]

By the time Tocqueville and Beaumont returned to France in 1832, *L'Avenir* had suspended publication because of episcopal disapproval; and later in the year the encyclical *Mirari Vos* made explicit Papal condemnation of mennaisian doctrine. During the next year, when Tocqueville and Beaumont were planning to launch a new journal, they discussed the possibility of securing Montalembert as a collaborator. It was not Montalembert's association with Lamennais in the "Avenir" movement that interested Tocqueville and Beaumont, but rather the fact that he was a person of some reputation who could work with them in the cause of "order and liberty." When the question arose of recruiting another former disciple of Lamennais, the Abbé Lacordaire, Tocqueville did not take exception to Beaumont's judgment that by involving themselves with Lacordaire and his friends "we would become involved with *l'Avenir* and all its theories: this isn't our concern."[11] Many years later, when Tocqueville wrote the *Souvenirs,* he referred to Lamennais as a "chimerical visionary," but he may have been referring only to the latter's position in 1848, long after his break with the Church.[12]

Nevertheless, Tocqueville's choice of phrase, taken together with Beaumont's remark, is suggestive. Tocqueville's image of himself throughout the period of the July Monarchy was that of an *homme politique,* always aware of the limits of the possible, particularly in the sensitive area of religious affairs. Lamennais was bolder, more intransigeant, impatient to promote wholesale change in the posture of the Church.[13] To Tocqueville this was indeed visionary, and he could feel no rapport or affinity. Probably, then, he was not influenced by Lamennais, and had arrived independently at some of the views associated with the "Avenir" movement. An ancillary problem, and one that will recur, is that of Tocqueville's relations with the more moderate followers of Lamennais, especially Montalembert. At this point, two remarks of a general nature can be made. First, unlike Montalembert, Tocqueville did not regard either his ideas or his conduct in political life as deriving from a specifically Catholic position. Given the problematic nature of his personal religious beliefs, this is almost self-evident. Second, he was always to keep his distance from Catholic political and social reform groups, especially when they were exclusively Catholic in membership or orientation. He was apprehensive about the effects of organized Catholic action on public opinion, since any intimation of Catholic power might well lead to renewed fear of Church domination, and thence to hostility towards Catholicism. The freedom of teaching campaign led by Montalembert was to have precisely this result, and confirmed Tocqueville in his opinion that Catholic action "en bloc" was a two-edged sword. Throughout the July Monarchy and into the years of the Second Republic he maintained an aloofness from the liberal Catholics, despite affinities of viewpoint and political stance.

Tocqueville's preoccupation with the need to reconcile Catholicism and liberal opinion in France followed from his belief that religion, and more specifically Christianity itself, retained its value and relevance. In 1843 he found himself engaged in an exchange of letters with Arthur de Gobineau on these matters, and because the younger man did not at all share his views, Tocqueville was forced into a frank and sustained defense of his position. Their correspondence was occasioned by a study that Tocqueville had agreed to prepare for the *Académie des sciences morales et politiques* on the subject of "Moral ideas of the nineteenth century and their application to politics and administration." Gobineau was acting as Tocqueville's research assistant, and at the outset the latter raised the question of whether "modern morality," that is to say the moral ideas of the Enlightenment and of the nineteenth century, should be considered as really new. The advent of Christianity had unquestionably constituted a revolution in morality, he wrote, because it gave first place to those values—humanity, pity, forgiveness—that had previously ranked last. By insisting that moral obligations extended to all, slaves as well as masters, Christianity also introduced the idea of human equality and fraternity. Finally, morality itself became purer and more disinterested because of Christian belief in the afterlife as the goal of existence and the sanction of moral laws. As for "modern morality," Tocqueville was clearly unconvinced that it had produced the same kind of fundamental revolution: "We have perhaps added nuances to the colors of the picture, but I don't see that the colors are entirely new."[14] Gobineau did not agree, and the protagonists were to continue to debate this point in subsequent letters.*

*In some respects their arguments oddly resemble those of Carl Becker and Peter Gay on the "newness" of the Enlightenment. The latter historian's strictures upon the methodological error of seeing nothing new under the sun are equally applicable to some of Tocqueville's statements. See Peter Gay, *The Party of Humanity* (New York, 1964), pp. 191-192, 208.

What was at issue for Tocqueville, however, was not primarily a question of historical interpretation, but the larger issue of the continued relevance of Christian morality. Taking for granted the value of the personal ethics taught by Christianity, he endeavored to prove to Gobineau that innovations in social morality derived ultimately from Christianity. He explained that the modern belief that all men have a right to the goods of this world, and that it is therefore the duty of the wealthy to aid the poor, developed out of the Christian idea of equality. And charity itself, which was originally a Christian private virtue, is now being extended into a public, or governmental, obligation. Tocqueville did admit that in one area, that of public morality, Christianity is weak, because it has neglected to define the duties of men as citizens, and to spell out their obligations to their country. With the growth of political passions these questions have become increasingly important, and therefore the modern world has been integrating the idea of public virtue, which was highly developed among the ancients, into the framework of Christianity.[15] In response to the changed political conditions of the Second Empire, Tocqueville was to become far less sanguine about the development of public morality, at least among the French, but he insistently affirmed that the duties of citizenship should be incorporated within the Christian moral code.[16] Fundamentally, his point of view throughout the correspondence was that beneficial innovations either derive from Christianity or, as in the case of citizenship, can be readily accommodated under its rubric. Undesirable changes in morality, on the other hand, were attributed to the loss of religious faith. For example, he described both the Saint-Simonian doctrine of "the rehabilitation of the flesh" and the Utilitarian tenet of "self-interest rightly understood" as reflections of the weakening of belief in an afterlife. This leads to a far greater emphasis on material needs and pleasures, while the sanction for morality comes to be found in this world.[17] There is a quiet contempt evident in Tocqueville's words as he describes these doctrines, both of which he adjudged to be mere varieties of materialism.

Gobineau countered with an unequivocal defense of the uniqueness and value of the morality that had emerged out of the Enlightenment. He compared the humanitarianism of modern morality—its concern for bettering the lot of the worker, the poor, the prisoner—with what he regarded as the excessive otherworldliness of Christianity. In addition, he criticized the Christian emphasis on faith rather than on works, concluding that the modern separation of religious belief from morality has had the happy result of ensuring religious freedom. The basis of this new morality, according to Gobineau, was a broader, more socially oriented, and psychologically sophisticated version of the eighteenth-century idea of self-interest properly understood.[18] But to Tocqueville the inherent superiority of Christianity was self-evident, and he was genuinely astonished by Gobineau's failure to agree that the Gospels express a purer, more spiritual code of ethics than that of any other moral system. As for the abuses and the exaggerations for which Christianity can be criticized, these were due to the milieu in which the religion was forced to live for many centuries, and not to its intrinsic principles. Tocqueville admitted that excessive "glorification of the spirit" is perhaps characteristic of Christianity. But does not Gobineau find "that there was an incomparable beauty in this open struggle of the spirit against triumphant matter?" He also agreed that the emphasis on faith rather than on works, which is to be found in all religions, does lead to intolerance. Nevertheless, the evil of intolerance is preferable to the state of affairs that ensues when morality loses the sanction of religious faith. Because he is convinced of the necessity of a positive religion, Tocqueville acknowledged frankly that he is less inclined than Gobineau to stress the disadvantage of even the best religion.[19] The transition from a defense of Christianity in terms of its inherent nobility to arguments of another, more pragmatic nature, was made without any apparent discomfort on Tocqueville's part.

In his rebuttal, Gobineau attempted to force Tocqueville to confront the inconsistencies and confusions in his mode of argument. This incisive research assistant made short work of Tocqueville's eulogy of the Gospels, remarking that although they were indeed moving, they should be understood as a superb popular distillation of the wisdom of the time. In other words, the emotional effect of the Gospels does not constitute proof of the uniqueness and superiority of Christianity. Nor can Christianity be singled out because of its moral teachings, since all religions preach virtue and advocate socially useful principles. At this point, Gobineau, who evidently possessed more temerity than tact, asked Tocqueville bluntly why, given his veneration for Christianity, he was not a believer. The explanation is that Christianity no longer has enough authority or strength to establish itself in his mind and feelings; reason, daily life, and the entire world as it exists, promote doubt and disbelief. This is unavoidable, but instead of accepting a new system of beliefs, Tocqueville is like Cicero, mourning the decay of the old and fearing that the new held no guarantee of social order. Is it impertinent to suggest that, for all his admiration of Christianity, Tocqueville is less concerned with its absolute truth than with its utility? As though to administer the coup de grâce, Gobineau concluded with the remark that even from a pragmatic point of view the beneficial effects of Christianity were questionable.[20]

Tocqueville's reaction to this extraordinary letter, which brushed aside the carefully wrought fabric of his religious views and ruthlessly exposed its weaknesses, can only be conjectured. Perhaps the most significant clue is that he intimated, gracefully but firmly, that he did not wish to continue the discussion. And, although he did answer some of Gobineau's more general arguments, Tocqueville completely ignored his young friend's attempt to engage him on the level of personal belief and attitude. He touched only fleetingly upon their differing evaluations of Christianity, writing that Gobineau was too severe in judging "this religion which has nevertheless contributed so much in putting us at the head of mankind."[21] On the question of the political utility of religion, however, Tocqueville was willing to express himself forcefully and explicitly. He reiterated his conviction that religion was essential to society: it is far likelier, he predicted, that if Christianity disappears it will be replaced by a new religion than that modern societies will prosper without religion.[22] And so Tocqueville brought this exchange of views to an end, remarking that because of his esteem and friendship for Gobineau he was distressed by their lack of agreement. Yet the reader leaves these letters with the feeling that the very lack of agreement, together with the challenging nature of Gobineau's comments, provoked an unusually enlightening dialogue.

This correspondence reveals the depth of Tocqueville's belief in the continued value and viability of Christianity. But what is notable is that he was forced to explain and defend his reasons for adhering to this belief. When arguing with Gobineau, the conventional pieties that prevailed in the "notable" society of the July Monarchy, at least in public discourse, did not suffice. Gobineau neither assumed that morality must be based on religion nor acknowledged the superiority of Christianity to all other value systems. In attempting to convince him of the validity of both of these propositions, Tocqueville was compelled to go beyond the kind of apologia for religion in general, and Christianity in particular, that is found elsewhere in his writings. He was franker and more incisive, although his arguments reflect the usual dualism between his personal sympathy for Christianity and his tendency to evaluate religion pragmatically. Gobineau, on the other hand, openly accepted the touchstone of social and political utility, and was manifestly impatient of Tocqueville's advances and retreats from this position. The consistency of Gobineau's approach serves to underline the extent to which Tocqueville "was painfully reluctant to eschew completely the conventional resort to arguments of a transcendental nature."[23] For Tocqueville these arguments were not merely "conventional"; they retained sufficient substance and meaning to make it impossible for him to reject them.[24] Accordingly, this exchange of letters reinforces the view that Tocqueville's defense of Christianity rested on personal, emotional grounds as well as on those of social and political utility. And this defense itself, with its unyielding affirmation that Christianity remained the source of all morality, public and private, explains his anxiety to bring about the reconciliation of Catholicism and modernity in France.

But what of Tocqueville's public life? How did his activities during the July Monarchy, especially in the Chamber of Deputies, relate to his religious commitments and concerns? In the case of the two parliamentary issues with which he was most closely identified—penal reform and the abolitionist movement—the influence of his religious position was evident, although not crucial. The investigation of the American prison system undertaken by Tocqueville and Beaumont resulted in their joint author-ship of *Du Système Pénitentiaire aux Etats-Unis et de son application en France,* published in 1833. This sufficed to mark the two men as "experts" on prison reform, and after their election to the Chamber both were active members of parliamentary commissions examining the problem. *Du Système Péniten-tiaire* is almost barren of material relating to religion, and even its few fragmentary remarks cannot be taken as altogether trustworthy evidence of Tocqueville's views, since it was, in fact, Beaumont who wrote the book.[25] The authors did note with obvious approval that "moral and religious instruction" was the basis of the American penal system, and they also took occasion to comment upon the obstacles that prevented the French clergy from aiding in prison reform. Their explanation of these phenomena presage the themes that were to be developed in the *Démocratie*: the "unnatural" prejudice against religion in France caused by the union of church and state, as opposed to the pervasiveness of religious influence in American society, where church and state are separated.[26] These are clearly more or less gratuitous remarks interjected by Tocqueville and Beaumont for the edification of their French readers.

Tocqueville's approbation of the "essentially religious" character of the American prison system found expression in the report that he submitted to a parliamentary commission on penal reform in 1840. He suggested that both the French clergy and religious laity should play a more active role in the prison reform movement, and he contended that religion could be the chief instrument of moral reform in the prisons.[27] In a speech delivered to the Chamber in 1844 he suggested that the rationale of the penal reform movement was fundamentally Christian. Belief in "rehabilitation following atonement" had been introduced by Christianity; despair of the possibility of reform was a return to paganism. But, he hastened to add, it was the French Revolution that had secularized these humanitarian ideas and applied them practically to law and administration. He had made the same point to Gobineau in their exchange of letters the previous year, but in this parliamentary address there is a slight shift of emphasis. Here, Tocqueville obviously wanted to stress the fact that although humanitarian ideas such as penal reform were Christian in origin, they had become thoroughly part of "the ideas of our time, of our age, of our civilization."[28] A pastiche of Christianity and of the glories of the Revolutionary heritage was more apt to produce sympathy in the Chamber than an excessive concentration upon the relevance of Christian doctrine and morality. What is most significant, however, is that the cause of penal reform, precisely because it exemplified the congruence between Christianity and "the ideas of our time," presented no problems or misgivings to Tocqueville, and he was therefore able to support it wholeheartedly.

Tocqueville played an important role in the French abolitionist movement, both within the Chamber and in journalistic endeavors designed to elicit popular support. Many of the arguments he marshalled in favor of the abolition of slavery in French colonies were of an economic nature, but he also introduced ideological and religious considerations.[29] In the *Démocratie* he had stated that slavery was incompatible with Christian ideas of human equality and fraternity, and that Christianity had suppressed slavery, only to see it reestablished in the sixteenth century.[30] The same point of view is implicit in the 1843 correspondence with Gobineau and it reappears in Tocqueville's abolitionist articles and speeches. Apparently the belief that Christianity had been responsible for the extirpation of slavery in Europe was "widely accepted" in the mid-nineteenth century, so that Tocqueville could expect this motif to be familiar and unobjectionable.[31] He argued that the impetus that had enabled Christianity to destroy slavery had weakened by the sixteenth century, but gained new vigor with the advent of "the modern French spirit." Specifically, the ideas of the French Revolution, by disseminating the concept of equality before the law, had reawakened the humanitarian impulse created by the Christian belief in equality before God. He even asserted that the British antislavery movement was really an expression of French principles.[32] Since abolitionism in France was suspected to being Anglophile, Tocqueville was at pains to show that its lineage was impeccably French and that it was the humanitarian ideas of 1789 that demanded the end of slavery in French colonies.[33]

In evaluating Tocqueville's activities in the abolitionist movement, Drescher concluded that "Rarely did liberty, equality, and religion so clearly converge in Tocqueville's perception, and where they converged he moved with seven league boots."[34] This statement is equally valid with respect to penal reform. Both causes were able to evoke a wholly sympathetic response from Tocqueville, since they were based upon a proper meshing of Christian morality and "modern ideas." Putting the matter somewhat differently, neither of these issues was divisive from the point of view of rapprochement between liberty and religion in France. Hence, in each case Tocqueville affirmed his position with decision and acted effectively. If, on the other hand, a political issue exemplified, not continuity between Christianity and Revolutionary principles, but the potential conflict between them, he was forced into a weak and ineffectual political stance. This was shown when he was confronted with the question of freedom of teaching, which agitated French political life during the 1840s.

The term "freedom of teaching" had been used in the revised Charter of 1830, where it was listed as a fundamental right to be secured to the French people as rapidly as possible by means of separate legislation. What this meant was that the monopoly over all educational matters enjoyed by the state and its creation, the Napoleonic University, was to be at least partially abrogated. The Guizot law of 1833 had fulfilled this promise as regards primary education, since it permitted the establishment and operation of private primary schools without government authorization and control. A bill that would have loosened the hold of the University over secondary education had been proposed by Guizot in 1836, when he was again Minister of Public Instruction, but it was withdrawn after his resignation the next year. In 1841 another bill was introduced into the Chambers by Villemain, Minister of Public Instruction in the ministry headed by Guizot, and this was the spark that ignited the freedom of teaching controversy. To most Catholics the projected law seemed not merely disappointing but retrogressive, since it included a provision that would extend government supervision to the only Catholic secondary schools hitherto exempt, the *petits séminaires*. Even the French episcopate, loath since the events of 1830 to take a position on political questions, publicly criticized the bill.

Although Villemain's bill was withdrawn, it had succeeded in arousing Catholic opinion to a sense of outrage and injustice. Montalembert in particular urged the formation of a "Catholic party," which would press for an acceptable freedom of teaching law. Catholic spokesmen and the Catholic press did not however limit themselves to demands that University control over secondary schools be removed.[35] Violent attacks on the "irreligion" and "immortality" of University teaching and teachers were frequent, especially after Louis Veuillot became editor of *L'Univers* in 1842. Not surprisingly, the University responded with its own accusations, most notoriously in the 1843 Collège de France lectures of Michelet and Quinet attacking the Jesuits. By the end of 1843 the question of control over secondary education, difficult in itself, had become embroiled in polemic and mutual recrimination. While the overt protagonists in the quarrel were the University and the "Catholic party," organized chiefly by Montalembert, it was really the right of the state to dominate education, and particularly the highly sensitive area of secondary education, that was at issue. Both Church and state were intensely concerned about the kinds of values taught in the secondary schools to those young men, primarily of the middle classes, who were destined to become the governing élite of France. How could freedom of teaching be reconciled with the felt need to use the lycées and collèges as a means of instilling either Catholic values or the values of post-1789 France? This was, and would remain, the crux of the problem as long as these two sets of values appeared to many in Church and state to be incompatible.[36]

In the last months of 1843 mention of the teaching controversy begins to be found in Tocqueville's correspondence. His comments centered about the ominous consequences of the prolonged and increasingly rancorous struggle. Instead of the sympathy and respect that marked public attitudes towards Catholicism in 1840, there is now almost universal hostility. As a result, the task of achieving harmony between the Church and modern society has been made immeasurably more difficult. He attributed primary responsibility for this situation to the "folies" of the Catholic party. Since the clergy had a just cause, it should have quietly and consistently demanded freedom of teaching in the name of the Charter. Gradually, the justice of its cause would have been acknowledged and its objective would have been gained. This was indeed Catholic strategy at the outset, but then influential spokesmen began to malign the University and its staff, and to suggest that the Church had the inherent right to supervise all education. The result has been to unnecessarily stir up all the old anticlerical doctrines and hostilities. Given the state of public opinion, Tocqueville feared that if the government presented a new bill dealing with secondary education the advocates of freedom of teaching, in whose company he placed himself, would be defeated.[37] Throughout the conflict his attitude was to remain unchanged: anxiety about the damaging effects of the controversy and advocacy of freedom of teaching on constitutional grounds.

Tocqueville's hope that the government would not introduce a new bill immediately was to be disappointed. There is no doubt that Guizot himself would have preferred delay or quiet negotiation with Catholic leaders. But political and party exigencies, which shaped Guizot's actions as they were to influence Tocqueville's position, did not permit delay. By the end of 1843 it appeared that customary party alignments might crumble and give way to new affiliations based on the freedom of teaching issue. The most powerful section of the dynastic opposition, led by Thiers and his associates, opposed freedom of teaching, either on principle or as a means of embarrassing Guizot's ministry, which theoretically favored it. And Odilon Barrot, the chief of that segment of the opposition with which Tocqueville was loosely linked, was moving towards alliance with Thiers on this issue. Many of Guizot's own supporters in the Chambers and in the press were equally hostile to Catholic demands. Thus, there seemed to be a strong possibility that if the education question could not be removed from the forefront of French politics the Guizot ministry would fall, to be replaced by a government led by Thiers. The Villemain bill of 1844 was a carefully constructed response to these pressures. It attempted to appease Catholic opinion by not interfering with the *petits séminaires*. But it maintained University supervision over private secondary schools, and it also prohibited members of unauthorized religious congregations, such as the Jesuits, from teaching.

A few weeks before the new Villemain bill was introduced into the Chamber of Peers, Tocqueville presented his own views on the education issue to the Chamber of Deputies. Much of his speech was clearly partisan, an effort on the part of a member of the opposition to charge the Guizot ministry with responsibility for "the philosophical and religious dissension" that was agitating France. Again and again he accused the government of inaction and weakness. The question of secondary teaching has been left unsettled for thirteen years; the existing educational laws should have been enforced or, if no longer applicable, should have been changed; the government has quietly allowed the prohibited religious orders to establish themselves in France, instead of committing itself to a decision about their legality. And, by doing nothing to check the violence and abuse of either the clericals or the *universitaires,* the government has exacerbated the quarrel over freedom of teaching.[38] After this catalogue of ministerial misdeeds or lack of deeds, Tocqueville turned from polemic to describe the effects of the prolonged controversy. Noting the increased hostility to Catholicism, he warned that the Church might resort to government protection, as a means of rescuing itself from weakness and isolation. If this occurs, France will be subjected to "the most detestable of all human institutions, a political religion, a religion serving the government and helping it to oppress men instead of preparing them for freedom."[39] Even if this calamity is avoided there remains the possibility that religion, bereft of public sympathy, would decay and eventually collapse. Tocqueville concluded with a homily upon the need for religious belief among a free people, observing that liberty is the daughter of *moeurs* rather than of institutions, while *moeurs* derive ultimately from religion.[40]

These Cassandra-like warnings are to the point and obviously deeply felt, but in the remainder of the speech Tocqueville offered few specific proposals designed to resolve the conflict. He did state that from the point of view of education, as opposed to instruction, the University was in need of reform. In the course of the debate he was urged by Villemain to define the kind of reform he had in mind, but Tocqueville did not comply. Two of the speakers who followed, and especially Corne, one of Tocqueville's political associates, did spell out these criticisms of the University in some detail. The crux of their argument was that the University has been more concerned with the scholarly abilities of its staff than with its capacity to impart "morale."[41] The distinction between education (the teaching of values) and instruction in various academic subjects was constantly stressed in Catholic attacks on the University, and Tocqueville took care to disassociate himself from these attacks. He insisted that he did not speak as an enemy of the University, explaining that he regarded lay education as the guarantee of freedom of thought in France. His purpose in criticizing the University was to strengthen it by means of reforms, and thus to enable public education to compete successfully with private schools.[42] There is every reason to accept these statements at face value, since Tocqueville's aim was indeed free competition among educational establishments, rather than a monopoly over teaching by either Church or University. But willingness to criticize the contending factions from Olympian heights could not provide a solution to real and knotty problems. To call for reforms within the University, for example, was not to make that all important decision regarding the extent of educational supervision to be entrusted to the University. There is justice to the criticism expressed by contemporaries (and reiterated recently), that in this speech Tocqueville sidestepped the basic issues in favor of edifying generalities and castigation of government policy.[43]

The fate of the second Villemain bill was ultimately to be the same as the first, but not until tensions and rancor had been heightened within the Chambers and, to a lesser extent, throughout the nation.[44] The debate in the Chamber of Peers—in which Montalembert called upon the sons of the Crusaders to go forth against the sons of Voltaire, and Cousin warned that the termination of University supervision over Catholic schools would divide France into two warring factions—did not help to calm the atmosphere. Eventually, the Villemain bill passed the upper Chamber, amended so that supervision of private secondary schools would be transferred from the University to the state. Despite this concession to Catholic opinion, the bill remained unacceptable to those Catholics who demanded freedom of teaching without any state control. It was equally unacceptable to those who believed that secondary education should be closely supervised by the University, representing the state. Tocqueville was a member of the commission appointed by the Chamber of Deputies to examine the Villemain bill, but the majority of its members were more sympathetic to the claims of the University than to freedom of teaching. Thiers was head of the commission, and the report that he presented to the Chamber in July was the analogue of Cousin's speeches in the upper Chamber: both flatly opposed the right of private secondary schools to operate without strict University controls over teaching staff and curricula. Because of the pressure of other business and the desire of the government to drop the matter, the parliamentary session came to an end in August without the report having been debated.

Tocqueville was extremely critical of the Thiers report, and especially of the way in which Thiers and his faction were using the teaching issue as a means of overthrowing the Guizot ministry.[45] He was aware of the increasing success of Thiers' strategy of coalescing the various segments of the dynastic opposition about "defense of the University" and denunciation of the Jesuits. It was at this time, in July 1844, that Tocqueville and some of his friends took over the direction of the newspaper *Le Commerce.* Part of his purpose in securing control of *Commerce* was to use it as a vehicle in the fight for freedom of teaching, but he also envisaged the newspaper as an organ of the opposition, which would be free to oppose Thiers on diverse questions of domestic and foreign policy. The outcome might be, as he well knew, the destruction of his political future. Tocqueville's willingness to take this risk was a measure of his contempt for the opportunism of those who were willing to stimulate the quarrel between the Church and the University in order to regain power.[46]

The pages of *Commerce*, from July 1844 until spring 1845, provide a means of fleshing out Tocqueville's views on the education question. The new direction of the newspaper set forth its views on this subject, and specifically on the Thiers report, almost immediately. The fundamental error of the report, according to *Commerce*, was its failure to realize that freedom of teaching is a right, and therefore should not be denied because the clergy and the legitimists wish to use it for their own ends. The University has been unjustly vilified, as the report states, and it is also true that those who stir up the clergy want to make a party of the Church and set it up as a rival power to the state. But after making these points, the commission should have gone on to grant freedom of teaching honestly and sincerely. Instead, it has proposed a bill that surrounds the rights to teach and to establish schools with a set of arbitrary and complicated conditions. If the freedom of teaching promised by the Charter is impractical or dangerous then it should be refused outright, rather than dishonestly eluded.[47]

About a month before the beginning of the new parliamentary session in which the Thiers report was to be discussed, *Commerce* took up the issue again, to distinguish its position from that of the other opposition newspapers. *Le Constitutionnel*, commonly considered to be the organ of the Thiers group, and *Le Siècle*, with which Tocqueville himself had been associated, but which he believed had come under the influence of Thiers, were singled out for criticism. Both newspapers were accused of occupying themselves too exclusively with attacks on the clergy, and particularly against the Jesuits. What is to be feared, *Commerce* comments, is not domination by the clergy, but rather the "shipwreck of belief" as a result of clerical excesses and the ensuing turmoil. In its obsession with the religious question the opposition was aiding the government strategy of diverting public attention from the more pressing problems of electoral reform and parliamentary corruption. Nor will resistance to freedom of teaching lead to defeat of the ministry, for the latter will not defend it, while the opposition will have violated its principles.[48]

47

Commerce then outlined its own policy, repeating that the exercise of the right of freedom of teaching could not be refused because it would be used to propagate unpalatable ideas. To oppose freedom of teaching from motives of fear is to emulate the attitudes of the legitimists and of the Restoration, and is a betrayal of the principles of 1789. Although *Commerce* disapproves of a state monopoly of education, it wishes to see more and better state schools, and believes that the government has the right to inspect all private educational establishments, including seminaries. All monopolies are dangerous, and only legislation that will really insure freedom of teaching can **provide** guarantees against uniformity and the arbitrary power of either Church or state. *Commerce* regards freedom of teaching as a benefit, while *Constitutionnel* and *Siècle* see it as a painful obligation imposed by the Charter.[49]

Although the thrust of its argument was that *Constitutionnel* and *Siècle* were betraying liberal principles in favoring a law that would make freedom of teaching "illusory," *Commerce* also castigated the behavior of the Catholic party, particularly that of *L'Univers* and of Montalembert.[50] To some extent this was a means of defense against accusations that *Commerce* was following the lead of Montalembert, the clericals, the legitimists, and *Univers*. Tocqueville himself was charged with having clerical and legitimist sympathies, but in deference to the feelings of Beaumont, who until this time had retained his association with *Siècle*, these attacks soon ceased.[51] None of the protagonists subjected the ostensible subject of the controversy—the Thiers report on the Villemain bill—to detailed examination. Given the complexity of both the original bill and of the report, this is perhaps not surprising, but the result was that much of the debate had the quality of shadowboxing. Nevertheless, since *Commerce* undoubtedly reflected Tocqueville's views on the education question, the polemic carried on in its columns provides a means of assessing the limitations, as well as the strengths, of his position.

After Villemain was replaced by Salvandy as Minister of Public Instruction in January 1845, the bill was withdrawn and the education issue lost some of its virulence. But in the spring a series of minor incidents led to a renewal of agitation, again focusing on the Jesuits. *Commerce* responded in its customary evenhanded fashion, criticizing the excesses and intolerance of the clergy, and yet insisting that the Jesuit threat was grossly exaggerated.[52] In May Tocqueville and his colleagues retired from the direction of *Commerce*, and their efforts to gain another journalistic forum failed. And gradually the circumstances that had led Tocqueville to risk personal attacks and political isolation ceased to exist. The success of the Rossi mission in July, and the subsequent more-or-less symbolic withdrawal of the Jesuits from some of their French houses, effectively defused the Jesuit issue. Thiers' strategy had been checkmated, and he ceased to occupy himself with the education question. In the parliamentary elections of the next year the Catholic party called upon its adherents to vote only for those candidates who favored freedom of teaching.[53] Tocqueville was among those who announced their support, but it is evident that his interest waned as the teaching issue ceased to be a focus of political and religious conflict.[54] When in April 1847, Salvandy, who remained Minister of Public Instruction in the Guizot government, introduced another bill, it encountered the familiar intransigeance of both Catholics and *universitaires,* but the bitterness and agitation of 1844 were no longer as pronounced. The end of the July Monarchy found the education problem still unresolved.

What can be concluded, then, from Tocqueville's response to the "alarums and excursions" of the teaching controversy? The most important point is that he was far more concerned with the effects of the controversy than with the issue itself. Freedom of teaching was desirable, but not at the cost of again polarizing France into clerical and anticlerical factions. Hence his willingness to concede that if the pledge contained in the Charter was impractical or dangerous, freedom of teaching should be categorically denied. Above all, the question had to be settled and cease to be an impediment to the goal of reconciliation between Catholicism and post-Revolutionary French society. His anxiety to avoid religious dissension explains Tocqueville's disapproval, not merely of the intemperance of the Catholic party, but of its very formation and existence. It might have been expected that the author of the *Démocratie en Amérique,* who had warmly praised the American capacity for group action and organization, would applaud Catholic efforts to act together in pursuit of a specified objective. Instead, he took every opportunity to berate Catholics for behaving as though they were members of a separate group, with its own principles, leaders, and interests.

Fréderic Ozanam expressed a similar point of view when he remarked that he was disturbed by the idea of a Catholic party because "then there would no longer be a Catholic nation."[55] Ozanam, a devout Catholic, was implying that if Catholics entered the political arena as a distinct group, it was an admission that they were only one group among many, that, in fact, most Frenchmen were no longer Catholics. Tocqueville went a step further, and saw that if Catholics called attention to themselves and acted as though they possessed actual or potential power, it would court hostility and therefore ensure that France would not be a Catholic nation. Although he never denied that Catholics had the same rights as other groups to press for their aims through the political process, he was also persuaded that only the greatest tact and restraint in the exercise of these rights could dispel the latent fear of clerical domination. Perhaps because he was always wary of any religious entanglement in politics, Tocqueville did not fully appreciate the fact that the Catholic party did take the unprecedented step of addressing itself to public opinion rather than to the government.[56] Nevertheless, his trepidation about the hazards of Catholic political action was to remain amply justified until after World War I.

On the question of freedom of teaching, Tocqueville's position was unambiguously in the liberal tradition of Constant, as opposed to the "statism" of the Doctrinaires. The latter feared that freedom of teaching would lead to the reestablishment of the Church's control over the schools, while their own aim was to use University-controlled public education as a means of national unification.[57] Tocqueville considered the threat of clerical domination to be a chimera; he believed that University monopoly of education was inconsistent with the competition among individuals and groups that ought to prevail in a liberal society. As Rémusat noted, Tocqueville's concept of educational organization derived from his "American liberalism," and hence he saw no incompatibility between freedom of teaching and a lay state.[58] He was aware that the American model could not be applied wholesale to France, and therefore assumed that the University would remain a state-supported institution, armed with supervisory powers over education. He had no illusions that freedom of teaching could be undertaken without risk, but he accepted the traditional liberal argument that liberty must not be denied because of the fear that it might be used for the destruction of freedom itself. From the point of view of political philosophy, Tocqueville's position was both consistent and a logical corollary of what Drescher has called his "Anglo-liberal" proclivities.[59]

In terms of French religious and political realities, this position could lead only to ineffectiveness and frustration. As tensions grew, the vocabulary of "Anglo-liberal" sentiments became increasingly irrelevant to those considerations of ideology and power that dominated the situation. Tocqueville did not give these factors sufficient weight: he persisted in thinking that were it not for malign or injudicious actions, the goal of freedom of teaching could be reached. Had circumstances forced him to put forward a proposal aimed at solving the crucial problem of the nature and extent of University regulatory powers, he might have come to realize that no solution could be found that was mutually acceptable to the Catholic party and to the *universitaires*. As it was, he spent himself in tireless denunciation of those who were inflicting religious dissension upon France, or he was reduced to edifying generalities about freedom and competition. Meanwhile, the ramifications of the issue itself were generating a divisiveness that made these principles inoperative, and which was exacerbated by the rhetoric of a Michelet or a Veuillot. Tocqueville was, in fact, confronted by a situation in which the obstacles to harmony between the Church and nineteenth-century French society were revealed with shattering clarity. In such a situation his views took on an air of unreality. When finally a compromise was reached, in the aftermath of the Revolution of 1848, it was motivated by fear of class conflict and not by devotion to the principles of liberty and competition.

Questions of poverty, unemployment, workers' rights—in short, that congeries of issues usually called the social question—did not play a central role in Tocqueville's political life. When, however, these problems did obtrude themselves upon his attention his religious orientation influenced his perceptions and attitudes. For example, much of the argument of the *Memoir on Pauperism*, which Tocqueville delivered to a provincial learned society in 1835, derived from the *Economie politique chrétienne*, published the previous year by Villeneuve-Bargemont, an early French social Catholic. In the *Memoir* Tocqueville described charity as being rooted in an instinctive desire to help the unfortunate, which Christianity then exalted into "a divine virtue." Public or legal charity, on the other hand, was the systematic effort of society itself to aid the needy.[60]

There is no need to recount the arguments that Tocqueville used to prove that legal charity has deplorable results; what is interesting is that they were a mélange of economic liberalism and of the nostalgic medieval corporatism characteristic of the conservative wing of French social Catholicism. Legal charity engendered class conflict, but almsgiving had the beneficial effect of establishing "moral ties" between the rich and the poor. Also, it is more degrading to ask for charity in the name of the law than to ask for pity "in the name of He who regards all men from the same point of view and who subjects rich and poor to equal laws."[61] The point is that Tocqueville who, unlike Villeneuve-Bargemont, was neither a devout Catholic nor a legitimist, was able to use such arguments without any apparent sense of embarrassment or anachronism. With at least one part of

51

his mind, the problem of poverty remained associated with Christian ideas of *caritas* and good works.

In the 1843 dialogue with Gobineau, Tocqueville's emphasis was somewhat different, since he was concerned with proving that modern ideas of charity and of social reform have their origin in Christian teaching. He did not express disapproval of the expansion of Christian charity into a public obligation, and he even expressed interest in learning more about the "right to work" doctrines of socialism. This does not necessarily mean that his opinions had changed, but merely that in his correspondence with Gobineau, his primary purpose was to demonstrate the continuity between Christianity and modern morality, and not to judge the latter. Nevertheless, during the last years of the July Monarchy, his attitude towards public assistance did become somewhat more flexible, as a result of his increasing concern with the revolutionary potential of the social problem. He was prepared to support legislation that would lower the tax burden on the poor, as well as other means of indirect aid, such as savings banks and schools.[62] These measures would, he hoped, improve the situation of the workers and halt the progress of socialist doctrines. His aversion to socialism itself, although not really spelled out until after the Revolution of 1848, was based on a kind of moral contempt, in addition to disapproval of its political and economic doctrines.[63] As he had remarked to Gobineau in the course of their 1843 dialogue, socialism was merely another form of materialism, or lusting after the goods of this world.

Tocqueville believed that the "notables," the directing and owning classes of French society, should join together in private efforts to help the poor, as well as to sponsor suitable legislation. In 1845 and 1847 he joined two groups that shared these objectives, the *Annales de la Charité* and the *Société d'Economie charitable*. Both of these were conservative social Catholic organizations, animated by the conviction of Armand de Melun that it was the duty of the upper classes to promote, organize, and strengthen private charity. And, by 1847, Melun was demanding that the legislature itself take a hand in investigating working-class conditions. The membership of both groups was exclusively "notable," and reflected the attitude of the "notables" to the social question. That is, there was willingness to recognize moral obligations on the part of the wealthy towards the poor, but not to recognize the "rights" of the poor to work or public welfare.[64]

It is difficult to assess the significance of Tocqueville's membership in these organizations, beyond the fact that he chose to associate himself with groups that sought social amelioration as an extension of the Christian principle of charity. Both organizations were nonsectarian: they presented no difficulties in terms of Tocqueville's ambiguous relationship to Catholicism or of his dislike of Catholic action "en bloc." Nevertheless, he appears not to have been particularly active in either of the Melun groups, possibly because their heavy concentration of legitimists made him wary of too close and visible an association. There were social Catholic organizations untainted with legitimism; for example, those of Buchez and Ozanam, but these were comparatively radical, since they spoke of "justice" as well as "charity," and of the "rights" of the workers as well as the obligations of the upper classes.[65] The paternalism of the conservative wing of French social Catholicism was far more compatible with the views on the social question that Tocqueville expressed during the July Monarchy. His failure to play a more active role in the Melun organizations reflects, not merely his fear of the legitimist stigma, but the fact that it was political, rather than social, issues that were able to elicit his sustained attention and commitment.

In evaluating the role of religion in Tocqueville's political life during the July Monarchy, it is impossible not to perceive an apparent disjunction between words and deeds, principles and practice. His assertion that he had entered public life to aid in the reconciliation of liberty and religion, even if not taken quite literally, was not rhetoric, but rather the corollary of his belief that religion was the basis of all morality. Unless Catholicism and modernity could come to terms, there was little hope that France could evolve into a stable and free society. These were the principles that Tocqueville wished to act upon as an *homme politique*. Yet, in the years before 1848 his political career was not distinguished by any great burst of activism on their behalf. This was partially the result of circumstances: much of Tocqueville's attention was devoted to questions of foreign policy and to the Algerian conquest, as well as to domestic issues unrelated to religion. More fundamentally, however, it was not the pressure of events, but the logical implications of his own theories and assumptions that precluded activism in the area of religious affairs. He was convinced that religious belief was a natural human instinct that would assert itself if impediments to its influence were removed. The most significant of these impediments was government control of religion, closely followed by clerical efforts to interfere in nonreligious matters. The Revolution of 1830 had loosened the ties binding Church and state, and had therefore opened the way to religious revival. And until the advent of the freedom of

53

teaching controversy, the French clergy seemed to be conducting itself with sobriety and tact. Hence, the scope of political activity was limited by the fact that the conditions necessary to strengthen religion and successfully integrate the Church into French society were present after 1830. Indeed, potentially divisive issues were best left undisturbed, since agitation served only to awaken dormant hostilities and reveal the fragility of the gains made since the Restoration.

Tocqueville's reading of the state of French religious and political affairs led to a defensive stance. He placed great emphasis, for example, on the need for vigilance to assure the continued separation of the spiritual and the secular powers, and he was ready to sound the alarm at the slightest hint of government manipulation of religion. An overt effort by the government to dominate the Church and use religion for its own purposes was, in fact, the kind of religious issue that would have aroused him to political activism. Tocqueville did not consider that the agitation of the Catholic party on behalf of freedom of teaching was justified, despite the fact that he favored the objective, because the result was anticlericalism and the subsequent weakening of religion. Defense of the conditions necessary to religious revival took precedence over the achievement of any goal that threatened to become a cause of religious dissension. He would never willingly expose such formidable matters as the Concordat, the organic articles, the position of the religious orders, as well as the education question itself, to protracted public discussion and controversy. In dealing with nonreligious issues there was no need for a purely defensive posture, and here he was free to set an example of action in public life that was liberal, sympathetic to religion, and yet not compromised by Catholic affiliations.

With respect to penal reform, abolitionism, and the social question, Tocqueville was able to invoke the continuity between Christianity and modern liberal humanitarianism. This was a matter of personal conviction, as the 1843 correspondence with Gobineau testifies; it was also a means of pleading the cause of reconciliation between Catholicism and post-Revolutionary France. In terms of the achievement of this goal Tocqueville tended to identify the task of statesmanship with the task of education. The statesman must make his fellow citizens realize the nature of the trial that confronted France, a trial both of the Church and of the society in which it existed. It was towards this end that Tocqueville bent his efforts, in his political life as in his writings. These efforts were to continue after the demise of the July Monarchy, although new circumstances would call forth changes in political practice.

Notes

1. Tocqueville to Corcelle, Nov. 15, 1843, *Oeuvres* (B), VI, p. 121.
2. Tocqueville to Eugène Stoffels, July 24, 1836, *Oeuvres* (B), V, pp. 432–435; Tocqueville, "Discours prononcé à la Chambre des députés sur la liberté religieuse," Apr. 28, 1845, in *Oeuvres* (B), IX, p.422. When discussing religion in France, Tocqueville sometimes refers explicitly to Catholicism and, at other times, uses the terms "religion" and "Catholicism" synonymously.
3. Tocqueville, "L'Etat social et politique de la France avant et depuis 1789," in *Oeuvres* (M), Tome II *(L'Ancien Régime et la Révolution)*, vol. 1, pp. 36, 53. This essay, first published in the *London and Westminster Review* in 1836, contains many ideas that Tocqueville was to develop in the *Ancien Régime.*
4. Tocqueville to Lord Radnor, May, 1835, *Oeuvres* (B), VI, pp. 44–50.
5. Tocqueville, "Discours prononcé à la Chambre des députés sur la liberté religieuse," Apr. 28, 1845, in *Oeuvres* (B), IX, pp. 419–420.
6. George Boas, *French Philosophies of the Romantic Period* (New York, 1964), ch. 3; S. C. G. Charléty, *La Monarchie de Juillet, 1830–1848* (Paris, 1921), pp. 105, 324–325; Adrien Dansette, *Histoire religieuse de la France contemporaine* (Paris, 1965), pp. 242–243; Adeline Daumard, *La bourgeoisie parisienne de 1815 à 1848* (Paris, 1963), pp. 347–351, 622–623; André-Jean Tudesq, *Les grands notables en France (1840–1849)* (Paris, 1964), vol. 1, pp. 124, 436.
7. Weill, op. cit., pp. 58–59.
8. *Oeuvres* (M), Tome V *(Voyages en Angleterre, Irlande, Suisse et Algérie)*, pp. 34–35, 50–51; see also Seymour Drescher, *Tocqueville and England* (Cambridge, 1964), pp. 71, 97, 126.
9. Tocqueville, "Discours prononcé à la Chambre des députés sur la liberté religieuse," Apr. 28, 1845, in *Oeuvres* (B), IX, pp. 419–421.
10. See Alec R. Vidler, *Prophecy and Papacy* (New York, 1954), p. 139.
11. Tocqueville to Beaumont, Aug. 13, 1833, *Oeuvres* (M), Tome VIII (op. cit.), vol. 1, p. 125; Beaumont to Tocqueville, Aug. 24, 1833, *Oeuvres* (M), Tome VIII (op. cit.), vol. 1, p. 128.
12. Tocqueville, *Oeuvres* (M), Tome XII *(Souvenirs)*, p. 180.
13. Vidler, op. cit., pp. 267–284, contains a balanced and sensitive evaluation of Lamennais' position vis-à-vis the Church.
14. Tocqueville to Gobineau, Sept. 5, 1843, *Oeuvres* (M), Tome IX (op. cit.), pp. 45–46.
15. Tocqueville to Gobineau, Sept. 5, 1843, *Oeuvres* (M), Tome IX (op. cit.), p. 47; also Tocqueville to Gobineau, Oct. 2, 1843, *Oeuvres* (M), Tome IX (op. cit.), pp. 60–61.
16. See ch. V.
17. Tocqueville to Gobineau, Sept. 5, 1843, *Oeuvres* (M), Tome IX (op. cit.),

p. 46; Tocqueville to Gobineau, Oct. 2, 1843, *Oeuvres* (M), Tome IX (op. cit.), pp. 58–59.

18. Gobineau to Tocqueville, Sept. 8, 1843, *Oeuvres* (M), Tome IX (op. cit.), pp. 49–55.

19. Tocqueville to Gobineau, Oct. 2, 1843, *Oeuvres* (M), Tome IX (op. cit.), pp. 57–59.

20. Gobineau to Tocqueville, Oct. 16, 1843, *Oeuvres* (M), Tome IX (op. cit.), pp. 64–66.

21. Tocqueville to Gobineau, Oct. 22, 1843, *Oeuvres* (M), Tome IX (op. cit.), p. 68.

22. Ibid., pp. 68–69.

23. Biddiss, op. cit., p. 621.

24. Biddiss seems to recognize this when he writes that Gobineau "seems the less shackled by conventional religious bonds" (op. cit., p. 624). Again, however, the use of the word "conventional" prejudges the issue.

25. See G. W. Pierson, "Le 'second voyage' de Tocqueville en Amérique," in *Alexis de Tocqueville: Livre du centenaire, 1859–1959* (Paris, 1960), p. 71.

26. Gustave de Beaumont and Alexis de Tocqueville, *Du système pénitentiaire aux Etats-Unis* (Paris, 1833), pp. 90–91, 105–106, 163–167.

27. Tocqueville, "Rapport fait au nom de la commission chargée d' examiner le projet de loi tendant à introduire une réforme dans le régime général des prisons," June 20, 1840, in *Oeuvres* (B), IX, pp. 307–308, 336–338.

28. Tocqueville, speech of Apr. 26, 1844 to the Chamber of Deputies, cited in Seymour Drescher, *Tocqueville and Beaumont on Social Reform* (New York, 1968), pp. 80–81.

29. See Seymour Drescher, *Dilemmas of Democracy. Tocqueville and Modernization* (Pittsburgh, 1968), ch. 6, for an analysis of Tocqueville's place in the French abolitionist movement.

30. *De la démocratie en Amérique*, vol. 1, p. 356, vol. 2, pp. 22.

31. David Brion Davis, *The Problem of Slavery in Western Culture* (Cornell, 1969), p. 18.

32. Tocqueville, "L'Emancipation des esclaves," from *Le Siècle* of Oct., Nov., and Dec. 1843; Tocqueville, "Intervention dans la discussion de la loi sur le régime des esclaves dans les colonies," May 30, 1845. These materials are in *Oeuvres* (M), Tome III *(Ecrits et discours politiques)*, pp. 88–89, 124–126.

33. Drescher, *Dilemmas*, pp. 159–160, discusses the prejudice against the abolitionist movement aroused by the belief that it was pro-English in sentiment.

34. Ibid., p. 190.

35. On the position of the Catholic press see Joseph N. Moody, "The French Catholic Press in the Education Conflict of the 1840's," *French Historical Studies*, VII, no. 2 (Spring 1972), pp. 394–414.

36. The literature on the teaching controversy during the July Monarchy is extensive, although much of it is far from impartial. The pages in Dansette (op. cit., pp. 246–256) provide a balanced summary. Among other works which should be consulted are the following: Louis Grimaud, *Histoire de la liberté d'enseignement en France*, Tome 6, *La Monarchie de Juillet* (Paris, 1954), pp. 11–18, 229–803; Paul Thureau-Dangin, *L'Eglise et L'Etat sous la Monarchie de Juillet* (Paris, 1880), pp.

98–460; Georges Weill, *Histoire de l'enseignement secondaire en France* (Paris, 1921), pp. 94–108; Weill, op. cit., pp. 77–85.

37. Tocqueville to Corcelle, Nov. 15, 1843, *Oeuvres* (B), VI, pp. 121–122; Tocqueville to Edouard de Tocqueville, Dec. 6, 1843, *Oeuvres* (B), VII, pp. 212–215.

38. Tocqueville, speech of Jan. 17, 1844 to the Chamber of Deputies, *Le Moniteur Universel*, pp. 92–93.

39. Ibid., p. 93.

40. Ibid.

41. Ibid., pp. 93–94.

42. Ibid., p. 92.

43. Drescher, *Dilemmas*, p. 113, note; Tudesq, op. cit., vol. 2, p. 713.

44. It is difficult to ascertain the extent to which public opinion was concerned with the teaching issue, at least until the parliamentary election of 1846, at which point analysis of voting patterns provides statistical data. The attitudes of the "notables" have however been carefully analyzed by Tudesq, op. cit., vol. 2, pp. 695–730.

45. Tocqueville was among the minority who had voted against Thiers becoming head of the commission, and hence its reporter. See Grimaud, op. cit., p. 673, also R. P. Marcel, *Essai politique sur Alexis de Tocqueville* (Paris, 1910), p. 200.

46. Tocqueville to Beaumont, Oct. 9, 1843, Dec. 27, 1843, Oct. 3, 1845, *Oeuvres* (M), Tome VIII (op. cit.), pp. 506–507, 525, 565; Tocqueville to Reeve, July 16, 1844, July 28, 1844, *Oeuvres* (M), Tome VI (op. cit.) pp. 75, 78; Tocqueville to Corcelle, Sept. 17, 1844, *Oeuvres* (B), VI, p. 124.

47. *Le Commerce,* July 29, 1844.

48. Ibid., Nov. 29, Dec. 3, Dec. 6, 1844.

49. Ibid., Dec. 3, 5, 8, 11, 1844.

50. Ibid., Dec. 3, 7, 1844, Jan. 15, March 8, 1845.

51. *Le Siècle,* Dec. 4, 5, 1844; *Le Commerce,* Dec. 8, 1844; see the lengthy note in *Oeuvres* (M), Tome VIII (op. cit.), pp. 543–545, for a discussion of these attacks.

52. *Le Commerce,* March 8, Apr. 15, 25, 27, 1845.

53. The best account of how this tactic affected the elections is in Tudesq, op. cit., vol. 2, pp. 709–710, 867–868; see also Daumard, op. cit., p. 610, and Patrick L.-R. Higonnet and Trevor B. Higonnet, "Class, Corruption, and Politics in the French Chamber of Deputies, 1846–1848," *French Historical Studies,* V, no. 2 (Fall 1967), pp. 204–224.

54. Tudesq, op. cit., p. 709.

55. Cited in Thureau-Dangin, op. cit., p. 191.

56. This is pointed out by Dansette, op. cit., p. 252.

57. One of the best statements of this point of view is to be found in Charles de Rémusat, *Mémoires de ma vie,* vol. 4 (Paris, 1962), pp. 67–71. Guizot gradually moved away from this position, however, and turned towards the Church as a bulwark against revolution. (See Johnson, op. cit., p. 145.)

58. Rémusat, op. cit., p. 44. The Catholic press also cited the example of the United States during the teaching controversy. (See Moody, op. cit., p. 407.)

59. Drescher, *Dilemmas,* p. 199, note.

60. Tocqueville, *Memoir on Pauperism,* cited in Drescher, *Tocqueville and Beaumont on Social Reform,* p. 11.

61. Ibid., p. 18.

62. Tocqueville to Dufaure, July 29, 1847, *Oeuvres* (B), VI, pp. 129–132. See also Drescher, *Dilemmas,* pp. 111–112, 204–206.

63. Tocqueville, *De la classe moyenne et du peuple,* Oct., 1847, in *Oeuvres* (B), IX, pp. 516–518; also Tocqueville, speech of Jan. 27, 1848 to the Chamber of Deputies, *Oeuvres* (M), Tome I, vol. 2, pp. 368–379.

64. See J -B. Duroselle, *Les Débuts du catholicisme social en France (1822-1870)* (Paris, 1951), pp. 217–227, 232–235; also Tudesq, op. cit., pp. 566–605.

65. Dansette, op. cit., pp. 270–272; Duroselle, op. cit., part I, ch. 2–3. Tocqueville seems not to have had any interest in, or knowledge about, the work of Ozanam and the *Société de Saint-Vincent de-Paul,* at least until after Ozanam's death in 1853. See Tocqueville to Ampère, Oct. 2, 1853, Nov. 18, 1853, *Oeuvres* (M), Tome XI (op. cit.), pp. 222, 227. And yet Ozanam shared Tocqueville's belief that religion should be kept absolutely separate from politics, resolutely maintained the nonpolitical stance of the *Société,* and, as has been noted above, disapproved of the aggressiveness of Montalembert and the Catholic party during the freedom of teaching controversy. The probable explanation is that Tocqueville's activities and interests moved only within "notable" circles.

Chapter IV

Religion in the Shadow of Revolution

Tocqueville had to some extent foreseen the imminence of revolution during the last years of the July Monarchy, so that his response to the events of February 1848 was chiefly one of anxiety for the future, rather than one of shock. He quickly decided upon adherence to the Republic and continued participation in political life, and he was elected a member of both the Constituent and Legislative Assemblies of the Second Republic. Animated neither by fervent approval nor by hostility in his attitude towards the new regime, he hoped that it could be guided into moderate and liberal channels. Above all, he wished to help steer the Republic away from the threat of socialism and then of Bonapartism. His fear of both was the mainspring that dominated his political life between 1848 and 1851. Within this short and crisis-ridden period Tocqueville exercised greater political influence than at any time previously, since his very lack of clear-cut partisanship was an asset. He was tolerable to the Republicans because he was not closely identified with the fallen monarchy, and he seemed honestly to accept the Republic. On the other hand, the powerful leaders of what Tudesq has termed "the counter-revolution which appeared at the same time as the revolution," had reason to think that Tocqueville did not oppose their aims. He maintained a loose affiliation with their organization, the rue de Poitiers committee.[1] But as Tocqueville approached the center of political power, particularly during his tenure as Minister of Foreign Affairs, his former independent stance could no longer be preserved, so that the actions of the *politique* do not always reflect the views of the *moraliste,* and the discrepancy between the two is apparent.

This was not, however, the case with regard to socialism. From the outset, Tocqueville's willingness to serve the Republic was linked to his fear of what was variously called "the Red Republic," "socialism," or "anarchism." All of these were emotion-laden terms used loosely by the propertied to describe their fear of social change. In an election address to his constituents less than a month after the Revolution, Tocqueville made it clear that he regarded "social order" itself to be at stake, and that he opposed alteration of property rights.[2] He argued against the inclusion of a "right to work" clause in the new constitution in a parliamentary speech which was, in effect, a root and branch condemnation of socialism. Disregard of property rights was one criticism, but Tocqueville also returned to the familiar accusation that socialism concerns itself only with material well-being. And he linked this moral critique to another of his bêtes noires: namely, that of the centralized and despotic state. The effect of socialism, he argued, would be to make men into insignificant dependents of an omnipotent state, retaining only the capacity for material gratification.[3] But so soon after the Revolution itself, and especially in the aftermath of the June Days, it would have been almost irresponsible to repudiate socialism and all its works without mention of any alternative means of solving the social problem. And so Tocqueville did admit that the state has obligations towards the poverty-stricken, and that it should help those who have exhausted their own resources. This, he insisted, was not socialism but merely "Christian charity applied to politics." It was not socialism, because he was not suggesting giving a "right" to government assistance to the workers, or putting the state in the position of destroying individual initiative by taking upon itself all decision-making. He concluded by defining the proper content of the Revolution of 1848 as Christian and democratic, but not socialistic.[4]

This speech reveals no deviation from the position that Tocqueville had taken during the July Monarchy, except that there is a more explicit approval of government action as a means of broadening the Christian principle of charity. He may have meant to imply that short-term assistance by the state in emergency situations was justified, particularly since large-scale temporary relief efforts were, in fact, undertaken by the Cavaignac government in the summer and fall of 1848.[5] But what of long-range, government-sponsored public assistance? It is clear that after the June Days all attempts at social amelioration did not come to an end. There were other options beside "the Red Republic" on the one hand and rigid repression on the other, and some of these possibilities were advocated by the very social Catholic groups with which Tocqueville was associated.[6] The most important of these was a measure that aimed at setting up a well-organized system of public assistance throughout France. It was introduced into the Assembly in November 1848 by Dufaure, the Minister of the Interior, with whom Tocqueville had close political ties during the Second Republic. This innovative plan had been influenced by Armand de Melun, but it never moved beyond discussion in either the Constituent or Legislative Assemblies. Tocqueville did not express an opinion on the Dufaure proposal. The only clue to his attitude is the fact that he was among the defeated minority that voted against a bill stating that a law on public assistance should be enacted before the Assembly dissolved itself.[7] Given the political situation, however, it is impossible to be certain that his vote was based upon opposition to the enactment of any national public assistance legislation. This bill came before the Constituent Assembly in the midst of the elections for the presidency. Tocqueville was convinced that Louis Napoleon would be the victor, and that this victory would weaken the Assembly as well as the Republic itself. Rapid dissolution of the Constituent and election of a new, presumably more conservative, Assembly might be a means of keeping Louis Napoleon in check. If this was indeed Tocqueville's reasoning, he would oppose any measure that implied prolonging the life of the Constituent. In this case, his vote does not serve as an indication of his attitude toward the Dufaure plan.

Government support of workers' cooperatives was also endorsed by Melun and the social Catholic movement, and a bill providing financial aid to these workers associations was accepted by the Assembly without debate or formal vote in early July 1848.[8] Again, there is no record of Tocqueville's attitude towards this legislation. He probably accepted it with resignation, as did many others in the period after the June Days.[9] In November, however, he joined the majority in refusing to accept a series of government proposals aimed at further support of the cooperatives.[10] The most likely supposition, in the light of what is known about his position on the social question, is that even the modest public assistance and social amelioration programs espoused by Melun were too "statist" to elicit Tocqueville's support.

An interchange with Nassau William Senior provides a glimpse of the indecisions and hesitations that beset Tocqueville when he attempted to come to grips with the social question. He stated unequivocally to Senior that France "must have a Poor Law," but then he expressed uncertainty about whether there should be a legal right to relief. The latter, he argued, must, by definition, be harsh and unpalatable to the recipients. If there is no legal right to relief (which must be hedged about with irksome conditions), assistance to those in need may be given "some of the attributes of real charity," and it can be made "a bond between the poor and the rich." He concluded with the standard complaint that the legal right to public assistance causes laziness and improvidence.[11] There is no effort at persuasion in this passage: Tocqueville was trying to explain his own inability to decide the merits of the case for public assistance. And what emerges is that as late as 1851 he still saw an incompatibility between "real charity" (that is, Christian charity) and a legal right to relief. Not surprisingly, Senior made no effort to reply to this aspect of Tocqueville's argument: it contained echoes of an organic, Christian social theory that Senior probably found meaningless or archaic. By this time, even the conservative wing of French social Catholicism represented by Melun had moved beyond this point, while Tocqueville continued to believe that in order for charity to remain *caritas*, it could neither be subsumed within an impersonal institutional arrangement nor considered as a "right" in legal terms.

This more-or-less emotional feeling on Tocqueville's part was only one factor influencing his attitude towards public assistance during the Second Republic. Nevertheless, it did serve to reinforce those arguments stemming from his acceptance of the precepts of economic liberalism and, most importantly, from his fear of "statism." Similarly, his assumption that the various forms of socialism were concerned with economic well-being to the detriment of human dignity and freedom meant that his critique was based not merely on political and economic arguments, but on deeply personal and ultimately religious grounds. There is no reason to doubt Tocqueville's seriousness or sincerity when he spoke of the need to apply Christian charity to politics. There is, however, ample evidence that his own doubts and fears prevented him from facing squarely the problem of what type of government action might be acceptable. And once the cataclysms of February and June 1848 were no longer in the foreground of his mind, his instinctive political priorities reasserted themselves.[12] Unlike Melun and the social Catholics, he was not led by his belief in Christian charity to any real examination of how this concept could be extended into a meaningful program of social amelioration.

During the fall of 1848 it became apparent that Louis Napoleon would be a candidate in the presidential election scheduled for December. As a result, Tocqueville's major concern shifted from socialism to the threat of

Bonapartism. He wholeheartedly supported the candidacy of Cavaignac, not just because the latter was preferable to Louis Napoleon, but because he believed that Cavaignac was capable of providing the leadership for a stable and orderly republic, once weaned from his erratic friends among the *républicains de la veille*. Many of those associated with the rue de Poitiers group, which was coming to be known as the "party of order," were uncertain as to who constituted the lesser of two evils—Cavaignac or Louis Napoleon. The election therefore presented the Catholic leaders within the party of order with the opportunity of throwing their support to the candidate who agreed to champion their objectives: freedom of teaching and, after the Roman Revolution of November, the temporal power of the Papacy. Neither Cavaignac nor Louis Napoleon could afford to ignore this strategy, since Catholic influence was far greater than it had been before the 1848 Revolution. Within the party of order the Catholic group was a more-or-less solid bloc, led by men who had demonstrated considerable skill in electoral organization during the July Monarchy. And the Church was no longer regarded with suspicion, but was eagerly accepted as an essential ally against further social upheaval. The classical expression of this changed attitude is to be found in the notorious remark of Cousin to Rémusat, immediately after the February Revolution: "Let us run and throw ourselves at the feet of the bishops; they alone can save us."[13] Both political expediency and fear of revolution united to give the Catholic group significant weight in the politics of the Second Republic.

The question of education had in fact presented itself as early as July 1848. At that time Hippolyte Carnot, the Minister of Public Instruction, had introduced a bill that would have removed some of the restrictions and regulations governing private (that is, chiefly Catholic) primary schools. To Catholic leaders, however, and indeed to most of the men of the rue de Poitiers, these concessions paled into insignificance beside the fact that the bill also provided for free, compulsory, and secular primary education. So great was the hostility to Carnot and his palpable attempts to use the schools as a means of instilling republican values that he was forced to resign almost immediately after the presentation of his bill. Tocqueville abstained from voting on the minor issue which became the occasion for a vote of confidence in Carnot, and which provided a significant parliamentary victory for the Catholics and for the party of order as a whole.[14] He did not abstain from this crucial vote out of sympathy for Carnot's ideas, but rather because he was unwilling to identify too closely

63

with the rue de Poitiers group and feared any weakening of the Cavaignac government.[15]

Although Carnot resigned after this parliamentary defeat, his education bill remained under study by a committee of the Assembly. The removal of this menace thus became the chief condition of Catholic support for Cavaignac's candidacy. Tocqueville's close friend and political associate, François de Corcelle, acted as intermediary in the ensuing, and ultimately fruitless, negotiations. Cavaignac was willing to postpone discussion of the Carnot plan or to modify it, but not to discard a bill of which he had approved. The result of the General's honesty and integrity was that Montalembert reached an understanding with Louis Napoleon and announced his support of the latter, who promptly began to take a sympathetic view of the Catholic educational position and of the temporal power. Immediately after his election to the presidency, Louis Napoleon offered the post of Minister of Public Instruction to Alfred de Falloux, one of the leaders of the Catholic group within the party of order. Falloux accepted the ministry with the specific aim of preparing a bill that would embody the Catholic definition of freedom of teaching.[16]

The Carnot plan was withdrawn and an extraparliamentary commission immediately began work on a bill designed to implement article nine of the new constitution, which provided for freedom of teaching. Among the members of the commission was Corcelle, whom Falloux considered to be neither an advocate of the University nor of the Catholic party, and therefore a neutral member of the commission.[17] Corcelle did not take a leading role in the commission's deliberations, limiting himself to the role of conciliator, a role for which he was uniquely equipped. His family background and political connections allied him to the liberals, while he had become an increasingly fervent Catholic and was trusted by the Catholic leaders.[18] By early June of 1849 the commission's work was complete, and Corcelle was chosen as the reporter of the bill to the Assembly.

In May of the same year elections to the Legislative Assembly were held. Although they resulted in a victory for the party of order, the more radical republicans demonstrated unexpected strength.[19] In an effort to reinforce the government against attacks from the newly revitalized left, Odilon Barrot, the head of the Council of Ministers, decided to liberalize the composition of the ministry. It was as a result of this ministerial reorganization that Tocqueville entered the cabinet, as Minister of Foreign Affairs. According to his own account, the post for which he thought

64

himself qualified was that of Minister of Public Instruction, but this was retained by Falloux. The latter did consider resigning from the cabinet because of its slight shift to the left; had he done so, Tocqueville would have been offered the education ministry.[20] Barrot's willingness to accept him for this delicate post is readily understandable, since Tocqueville was known to be a proponent of freedom of teaching, and yet he could not be considered a vehement partisan of either Church or University. Tocqueville's perception of himself as being both knowledgeable and potentially effective in this area is somewhat surprising, since he had never been particularly active or influential in educational affairs. In any case, he was never to be given the opportunity to assume real responsibility in this area.*

In the *Souvenirs* Tocqueville made it clear that his attitude towards the Falloux bill was determined by political considerations. Upon his entry into the ministry, he apparently advised his colleagues to allow Falloux complete latitude within his own department, although this entailed "great sacrifice."[21] This proposal was accepted, and Falloux was allowed to proceed with the preparation of his education bill and present it to the Legislative Assembly on June 18, 1849.† Only in this way, Tocqueville believed, could the ministry hope to gain the support of the legitimists and of the Catholics against Louis Napoleon, should the latter attempt to set aside the constitution and increase his own power. He did not explain the nature of the "sacrifice" entailed in allowing Falloux carte blanche, although this may be an oblique reference to his disapproval of Falloux's punitive attitude towards the University.[22] But whatever the nature of Tocqueville's apprehensions regarding the designs of Falloux and his Catholic and legitimist allies on the French educational system, they had to be thrust into the background in order to obtain the support of these powerful groups against the ambitions of Louis Napoleon. Curiously, Tocqueville's political realism did not suggest to him that once passage of the Falloux bill was assured, loyalty to the ministry and to the Republic might rapidly evaporate.

*This was the second, and last, occasion upon which Tocqueville almost secured the portfolio of public instruction. The first occurred in October of 1848, when Cavaignac decided to admit to the cabinet those who were not *républicains de la veille*. Tocqueville was suggested for the post of Minister of Public Instruction, but the cabinet was adamantly opposed. On this episode see: Tocqueville to Beaumont, Oct. 11, Oct. 12, 1848, *Oeuvres* (M), Tome VIII (op. cit.), vol. 2, pp. 59–65; *Souvenirs*, pp. 277–278.

†It was Falloux himself, and not Corcelle, who acted as the reporter for the commission's proposals, since Tocqueville had appointed Corcelle as special emissary to the Pope.

Although he was primarily concerned with the political expediency of the Falloux bill, rather than with its intrinsic merits or flaws, this is not to imply that Tocqueville found its proposals largely unsatisfactory. Some of its provisions did loosen University control over the operation of both primary and secondary schools and thereby conceded increased freedom of teaching. But the power of the University to govern itself was also sharply reduced, since many of its administrative and supervisory functions were put into the hands of civil servants and "notables." And the implications of various provisions of the text was that members of unauthorized religious congregations (that is, the Jesuits) were to be allowed to teach.[23] The fundamental assumption underlying the bill was that Church and state were mutually concerned with education, and that a new definition of the respective prerogatives of each was necessary. Fear of revolution, together with a feeling that the University was somehow responsible for the doctrines that had caused social upheaval, resulted in a readiness to allow the Church greater influence in educational affairs. But, and it was the extremist Veuillot who recognized this as well as some of the republicans, the Falloux bill did not free Church schools from state supervision. Instead, it made the conditions of surveillance less onerous. The yoking together of Church and state in matters of education was, in the last analysis, a reflection of the ties between Church and state imposed by the Concordat.

Ultimately, on a level beneath that of political expediency or of response to its various provisions, Tocqueville's acceptance of the Falloux bill meant willingness to maintain the existing structure of French church–state relationships. Immediately after the February Revolution, there were rumors that clerical salaries would be suppressed and complete separation of church and state introduced. Tocqueville remarked to Senior that he was opposed to depriving the members of the clergy of their salaries, and that if their stipends could be increased, more capable men would enter the Church.[24] While this comment does not address itself to the principle of separation, it does indicate a desire to preserve the status quo. The question of clerical salaries and of state supervision over religious groups arose during the deliberations of the committee that drafted the constitution of the Second Republic. Tocqueville, who was a member of this committee and present when these matters were discussed, neither spoke nor intervened in any way.[25] He did not choose to take the unique opportunity presented by the creation of a new constitution to press for separation "à l'Amérique." Evidently, he shared the feeling of the majority of the commission that however admirable separation of church and state might be in theory, it could not be introduced into France without grave risk.[26] The constitution of the Second Republic did not change the legal position of the Church, or indeed of any other religious group. The corollary in terms of education was obvious: the perennial quarrel over freedom of teaching would be resolved by means of compromise and mutual concessions, since breaking the bonds between church and state had been judged impracticable.

During the summer of 1849 the journals of the left and the *universitaires* gave vent to their opposition to the Falloux bill. The journals of the right and of the Catholics were more-or-less favorable, although Veuillot and his followers expressed outright opposition. But, excepting those with specific interests or principles at stake, the country at large did not appear to be aroused by the issue.[27] As for Tocqueville, he made no public statement about the bill, even after the dismissal of the Barrot ministry in late October 1849. The bill began threading its way through the Assembly during the same month, and it was not voted into law until March 15, 1850. Tocqueville was frequently absent from the Assembly because of illness during this period, and this in part accounts for his silence. The more basic reason, however, is that he continued to regard an education bill which more-or-less reflected Catholic preferences as politically indispensable. By arbitrarily dismissing a ministry that had not lost the confidence of the Assembly, Louis Napoleon had confirmed Tocqueville's suspicions. Therefore, it was essential to unite legitimists, Orleanists, and moderate republicans against further presidential encroachments. Enactment of the Falloux bill, whatever its deficiencies, was a small price to pay to prevent destruction of the Republic. From this point of view, speechmaking and discussion were beside the point, since necessity dictated passage of the bill with a minimum of recrimination and difficulty, if not with enthusiasm.

Tocqueville's voting record during the legislative discussions of the bill, although it is incomplete, corroborates this interpretation. In early November the question arose of whether the bill should be sent to the Council of State for examination before being discussed in the Assembly. The Catholic leaders were opposed, fearing that the Council would either make undesirable changes in the bill or postpone action upon it. The situation was complicated by the fact that Parieu, the new Minister of Public Instruction, had announced that if the Falloux proposals were sent to the Council, he would introduce legislation aimed at placing primary school teachers under stricter government surveillance. To many members of the conservative majority this was the crucial feature of the Falloux bill, rather than increased freedom for Catholic education. Hence, they were willing to shelve the earlier proposals in favor of Parieu's alternate, and simpler, legislation. The result was that Catholics and conservatives broke ranks, and the motion to send the Falloux bill to the Council of State was carried by a majority of one. Tocqueville voted against the motion, together with Montalembert and the Catholic group.[28] The consternation of the latter as a result of this development proved to be unjustified: the Council made few changes in the bill and finished its work by the end of December. At the time, however, the vote was in effect a test of loyalty to the Falloux bill as a whole, and of the priority to be accorded the Catholic demand for freedom of teaching.[29]

Before the vote on the Parieu primary education measure took place, it had become evident that the ministry was not trying to delay consideration of the Falloux bill. The customary alliance between the Catholic group and the conservatives reasserted itself, and the measure was ratified. Tocqueville nevertheless abstained.[30] This indicates, at the very least, lack of enthusiasm for a bill that was in fact harsh and punitive, and that placed the *instituteurs* thoroughly under the control of the préfects. Although he would not vote against it because this would mean allying himself with the left, he was willing to separate himself from the Catholic and conservative bloc when the fate of the Falloux bill itself was not at issue.

Tocqueville also chose to abstain rather than vote with the majority on two amendments to the Falloux bill. The first of these sought to make mandatory the existence of an *Ecole normale primaire* in each département, chiefly as a safeguard against an article of the bill that made possible arbitrary suppression of these state training schools. Both the Catholic leaders, who wished to strengthen Catholic primary education, and the conservatives, who looked upon the *Ecoles normales primaires* as veritable spawning places of socialism, were opposed to the amendment. Hence, the usual coalition prevailed, with such erstwhile supporters of the University as Thiers and Rémusat voting against the amendment, together with Montalembert and even Corcelle. But again, Tocqueville's dislike of measures that were animated solely by hostility to the University led him to register his disapproval by abstention.[31] The Bourzat amendment, which would have prohibited the Jesuits from teaching in France, raised a real possibility of dividing the majority. But Thiers, who in 1844 and 1845 had denounced the Jesuits and called for their expulsion from France, delivered an impassioned speech opposing the amendment. The majority held firm and the amendment was defeated. Tocqueville's abstention put him in the unfamiliar company of Victor Hugo and Lamennais, among others.[32] It was, nevertheless, consistent with the position he had taken during the July Monarchy, and in addition it did not endanger passage of the Falloux bill.

Despite the bill's flaws, it seems likely that Tocqueville would have voted for its enactment in the final decisive tally of March 15, 1850. He was not present in the Assembly throughout March because of illness, but on February 26 he voted with the majority in favor of going on to the third and final reading of the proposed legislation.[33] Had he been present on March 15, he might again have abstained, thereby registering his disapproval of certain provisions of the bill. Many of his closest political colleagues, including Beaumont, Lamoricière, and Odilon Barrot, did abstain, while Corcelle voted for the bill.[34] In any case, Tocqueville's voting record confirms the impression that he was not prepared to take any action that might impede passage of the bill, although he had reservations about certain of its features. Apparently, he regarded those provisions that were motivated by hostility towards the University as meretricious. He did not believe that public education should be penalized and weakened on the grounds that its teachings were allegedly a threat to social order. In this respect, his position differed from that of many conservatives (of whom Thiers was the prototype) who wished to strengthen Catholic education as a bulwark against further social disruption.

For Tocqueville the law was a measure dictated by political expediency and rendered more-or-less palatable because it did increase freedom of teaching. Like Barrot, he thought of it as a "treaty" between Church and state; he may have shared Barrot's belief that given changing circumstances it might well prove to be ephemeral.[35] But the Falloux law endured, and came to be perceived as both an engine of war against the University and an instrument of political conservatism. Thus, it ultimately caused increased divisiveness and antagonism towards the Church.[36] These consequences became apparent in the last years of the Second Empire and during the Third Republic: Tocqueville was spared the bitter knowledge that he had acquiesced in the passage of a law that widened the breach between liberty and religion in France. But within a short time, he was to learn that even from the point of view of immediate political advantage, the law had not served its purpose. Catholic support against the ambitions of Louis Napoleon proved in the event not to be forthcoming. Whether Tocqueville later regretted his part in the enactment of the Falloux law is not known. He may have considered the extension of freedom of teaching to be sufficient justification for the course he had followed. Ironically, it was precisely those portions of the bill about which he had misgivings, but which he did not criticize for reasons of political expediency, that eventually excited animosity against both the law itself and the Church.

The other testimonial to Catholic influence during the Second Republic was the restoration of Papal sovereignty by means of French military action in the summer of 1849. Since Tocqueville was Minister of Foreign Affairs at this time, he was directly and decisively involved in this complex and important diplomatic episode. Immediately after the Roman Revolution of November 1848, which made the Pope virtually a prisoner in Rome, there had been the possibility of French intervention. Cavaignac was prepared to send troops to Rome with orders to protect Pius IX, but not to interfere in the political situation. Meanwhile, Corcelle was sent as emissary to the Pope, offering protection and sanctuary in France. Pius IX, however, took refuge at Gaeta, in Naples. As soon as Cavaignac learned this he countermanded the order sending troops to Rome.[37] Tocqueville approved of Cavaignac's efforts to assure the safety of the Pope, although he was fearful that the presence of French troops at Rome might lead to complications. He thought that the best course would be to persuade the Pope to seek asylum in France. Judging from remarks made much later, Tocqueville seems to have hoped that Pius IX would promulgate necessary reforms once in France, and thereby open the way to peaceable termination of the Roman Revolution.[38]

On the eve of the French presidential election of December 1848, the Roman Republic set up by Mazzini and Garibaldi was still in existence, while the Pope remained in exile at Gaeta. Under Montalembert's prodding, Louis Napoleon publicly proclaimed his support of the temporal power, but immediately after his electoral victory he was not called upon to redeem whatever pledges he had made to the Catholic leaders.[39] It was only in late March 1849, after the defeat of Piedmont by Austrian troops at Novara, that Italian affairs took on a new urgency. The French were convinced that only the prompt dispatch of troops could prevent an Austrian march on Rome and subsequent Austrian domination of the entire Italian peninsula. And so the moribund Constituent Assembly authorized military intervention, but without clarifying the crucial question of whether the French army was to defend the Roman Republic or to restore the temporal power of the Papacy. As Falloux remarked, in what was surely an understatement, the resolution accepted by the Assembly "intentionally lacked precision."[40] For the Catholic faction, restoration of Papal sovereignty was the object of the expedition, while the

70

republicans had no doubt that they were acting to save a sister republic from imminent destruction. Louis Napoleon and Barrot were concerned with forestalling Austrian intervention: they believed that French occupation would protect Rome from a repressive restoration.[41]

The repulse of the French army before the gates of Rome on April 30 put an end to illusion. The successful attack with which the Romans had greeted their French "liberators" could not be viewed as apathy about the fate of the Roman Republic or readiness for French occupation. In the Assembly the republicans, furious at having played into the hands of the Catholic faction, demanded assurance that the expedition would not be used against the liberties of the Roman people. Nevertheless, Louis Napoleon took the position that French military honor now required a successful assault on Rome, and he pledged reinforcements for this purpose.[42] The conservative victory in the May elections to the Legislative Assembly left no doubt that military seizure of Rome, followed by Papal restoration, were to be the aims of French policy. It was at this point that Tocqueville entered the reconstituted Barrot ministry, to be flung into all the contradictions and entanglements of the Roman Affair.

Because he had been absent from France in the spring of 1849, he had taken no part in the Assembly's authorization of the Roman expedition. Before entering the cabinet, Tocqueville was questioned by Falloux about his attitude towards the intervention. He replied that had he been a member of the preceding ministry he would have opposed sending troops until the Roman people had been consulted about the temporal power. According to Falloux, Tocqueville went on to explain that since the French army was already at Rome the expedition had to be carried through. Only French occupation of Rome could prevent the entry of Austrian, Neapolitan, and Spanish troops. These comments reassured Falloux, who had feared Tocqueville's "sentiments américains" on the Roman question.[43] But Tocqueville's explanation is puzzling. If he was convinced that French national honor or interests made it imperative to prevent other military forces from entering Rome, then approval of French intervention would seem to be the consequence, regardless of the attitude of the Romans toward the temporal power. Immediately after taking office, Tocqueville learned that the order for an attack on Rome had been dispatched three days previously. In the *Souvenirs* he expressed sharp disapproval of this decision.[44] Yet it was the logical result of the conviction, which he himself shared, that occupation of Rome by French troops was essential. And despite his refusal to assume responsibility for actions taken prior to his entry into the cabinet, there was to be no change in policy. The assault on Rome began on June 4, two days after the new ministry came into office. Early the next month the Roman Republic came to an end when the French army entered the conquered city and proclaimed the restoration of the temporal power.

According to his own account, Tocqueville's Roman policy was governed by fear of increased Austrian influence in Italy and belief that it was necessary to repudiate all of the European revolutionary movements, lest they lead to renewed uprisings within France.[45] This meant willingness to preside over the destruction of the Roman Republic and to accept restoration of Papal sovereignty.* All of the evidence indicates that at this time he was sincerely convinced that the existence of the temporal power guaranteed the continued independence of the Church. It was in the interests of France and of all Catholic nations to protect the territorial dominions of the Papacy, because the spiritual functions of the Church would suffer if the Papacy became subject to diverse political and diplomatic pressures.[46] In one of the debates in the Assembly on the Roman question this position was criticized by Frédéric Arnaud (de l'Ariège), who called for the renunciation of the temporal power in the name of the spiritual influence of the Church. Arnaud was one of those few intrepid social Catholics who had refused to follow Montalembert and the majority of Catholics into the party of order.[47] On this occasion he argued that the buttressing of the repressive Papal regime was hindering the alliance of democracy and Catholicism. Nor would it be possible to obtain liberal reforms from Pius IX, since a true constitutional government was incompatible with the existence of the temporal power. Arnaud therefore called for the dissolution of the Papal States, while insisting upon the importance of Catholicism in modern, democratic societies.[48] Perhaps these words aroused some discomfit and second thoughts in Tocqueville's mind, for in his rejoinder he remarked that "for the present," the temporal power was necessary to preserve the independence of the Church.[49] Less than ten years later he was to reverse himself and decide that the spiritual independence of Catholicism was not contingent upon the existence of the Papal States. He explained to Corcelle that he was now able to consider the question "in the abstract," surely an oblique admission that during the

*Tocqueville's letters to his friend and translator, Henry Reeve, in June and July 1849, are an attempt to explain—and justify—this policy. See Tocqueville to Reeve, June 30, July 5, July 19, 1849, *Oeuvres* (M), Tome VI (op. cit.), pp. 101–107.

72

years of the Second Republic his judgment had been influenced by political and diplomatic exigencies.[50]

Even when he was foreign minister Tocqueville's advocacy of the temporal power was linked to insistence upon reform and modernization in the Papal States. In the Assembly he stated unambiguously that the restoration of Pius IX was not an end in itself, but that it must be accompanied by fundamental reform. This was essential to the very maintenance of the temporal power: to preserve and expand the moral strength of Catholicism, the Church must take care not to separate itself from the spirit of the epoch. What France was asking, Tocqueville explained, was that the Pope persevere in his efforts to heal the breach between modern ideas and the Church. The reforms initiated by Pius IX before the Roman Revolution resulted in religious revival, and they should be continued and extended.[51] These remarks cannot be dismissed as mere rhetoric meant to placate uneasy or hostile members of the Assembly. Both publicly and in his instructions to the various French representatives at Rome and Gaeta, Tocqueville persisted in demanding a specific set of reforms. Among the suggested political and administrative changes were creation of a legislative body with more than advisory powers; introduction of the Code Napoléon; secularization of the administration; and reorganization of the judicial system. In addition, Tocqueville regarded a generous amnesty as an indispensable means of reconciling the Pope with his subjects.[52]

By the end of August it had become apparent that the conception of reform held at Gaeta bore no resemblance to French demands. Furthermore, Pius IX was in an excellent position to resist the demands of his "liberators," since the restoration of Papal government was a fait accompli.[53] Admonitions that failure to undertake meaningful reform would result in antireligious feeling throughout the Catholic world were more indicative of Tocqueville's own fears than of the concerns of the Papal court. Nor did hints that France might publicly disavow responsibility for the restoration prove to be effective.[54] The publication of Louis Napoleon's letter to Edgar Ney in September clarified the extent of the president's disapproval of Papal policy, and Pius IX finally issued a statement of the reforms he was prepared to accept, together with a declaration of amnesty. Both documents were manifestly unsatisfactory, the *Motu Proprio* amounting to little more than a travesty of political rights, while the amnesty was in the nature of a proscription.[55] Tocqueville gave vent to his disgust and disillusionment with Papal policy in his correspondence with Beaumont, then ambassador at Vienna. At the same time he pressed Corcelle, the French envoy at Gaeta, to demand modifications of both the *Motu Proprio* and the terms of the amnesty.[56] Publicly, however, in what was to be his last address to the Assembly on the Roman question, he was far more sanguine. The cabinet did not wish to countenance the sentiments that Louis Napoleon had expressed in the Ney letter because it was suspicious of the president's motives, and it was unwilling to antagonize the influential Catholic group. Accordingly, in the October debate in the Assembly Tocqueville contented himself with mild criticism of both the *Motu Proprio* and the amnesty, and with expressing the "hope" that French demands would be met.[57] The ministry's position gained the support of the Assembly, but at the cost of presidential displeasure. Louis Napoleon did not yet have sufficient strength to punish the Assembly for its disregard of his wishes, but was able to dismiss a cabinet that had won "a victory at his expense."[58] He proceeded to accomplish this on October 31.

Discussing the Roman Affair with Senior two years later, Tocqueville stated that if the Pope had remained obdurate in his refusal to grant concessions, the Barrot ministry intended to issue a public protest and then to withdraw French troops from Rome.[59] Since Louis Napoleon himself could not effect any change of policy, it seems highly unlikely that the course of action Tocqueville described could have been carried out. Loss of Catholic support at home and Austrian troops in Rome were possibilities that neither president nor ministry nor Assembly cared to contemplate. For Tocqueville the fact that liberal reform did not result from the French intervention meant that "the whole expedition was a lamentable failure."[60] He had staked much of his intellectual capital on the premise that the reconciliation of liberal ideas and Catholicism was not only desirable but feasible. Reform within the Papal States was therefore not only an end in itself, but a crucial battle in the effort to accommodate Catholicism to the ideas of post-Revolutionary Europe. If the Pope showed himself willing to undertake change in his own dominions, which had seemed to be the case until the outbreak of the Roman Revolution, his example would leave only minor skirmishes to be fought against recalcitrant members of clergy and laity. The remaining years of this long Pontificate were in fact to be bleak and frustrating for any species of liberal Catholicism, in large part because of the burden of Papal disapproval.

Tocqueville's role in the Roman Affair was governed by the same considerations that determined his attitude towards the Falloux bill. In both cases political exigency circumscribed the extent to which his own moderate, but liberal, views could be put into action. As he came closer to the decision-making center of government, he too experienced the inevitable discrepancy between the principles of the *moraliste* and the demands of practical politics. The latter required gaining the support of the powerful Catholic faction against the ambitions of Louis Napoleon. To do this it was necessary to forward Catholic aims with respect to education and the restoration of the temporal power. Ultimately this strategy failed, and witnessing the alacrity with which the Catholic leaders allied themselves to Louis Napoleon was probably the bitterest experience of Tocqueville's political life.

His assessment of the behavior and position of the Church during the Second Republic did not prepare him for the readiness of Catholic clergy and laity to turn from republic to empire. Although he harbored no illusions that the spectacle of priests blessing trees of liberty should be taken at face value, he was persuaded that after February 1848 the Church enjoyed a prestige and influence that it had never been able to muster during the July Monarchy.[61] In describing the early days of the Revolution, Tocqueville explained that it was not affection that brought together the priests, the aristocracy, and the people in 1848, but rather a shared feeling of revenge against the middle classes and the July Monarchy. Regardless of motivation, however, the crucial facts were that the Church showed itself willing to accept the Republic, the clergy exercised its new influence with tact, and the antireligious feeling that had characterized previous revolutions was absent.[62] He was well aware that it was the shock of revolution and the attendant threat of socialism that produced a changed attitude towards the Church. Just as the events of 1789, and especially those of 1792, had cured the aristocracy of irreligion, so after February and June of 1848 the frightened middle classes came to realize the need for religious restraints, and wished to promote Christianity.[63] Tocqueville's judgment that fear of social upheaval provided the spur to alliance between the property-holding classes and the Church was valid. But his personal response to this phenomenon was ambivalent and somewhat puzzling.

When he described the changed religious situation to Senior, emphasizing that all except the lowest classes now adhered to Christianity, Senior denigrated the importance of this kind of "political faith." The "respect" or "conformity" that it produced concealed "general unbelief," according to Senior. Tocqueville did not reply to this criticism, arguing instead that it was not a question of "general unbelief," since "the instinct which leads the mass of mankind to assume the existence and the influence of a superna-

75

tural Being is so strong that it will always prevail unless it is violently opposed." Hence, if a religion is constantly preached and taught, "and treated by all the educated portion of society as if it were true," it will be accepted "by nine-tenths of those to whom it is offered."[64] These sentences display Tocqueville's tendency to assume the normality of faith and the way in which he obscured the distinction between religious belief and religious utility. He did not explain, for example, whether those men of property and education who were industriously fostering Christianity themselves accepted it as divine truth. The implication of this remarks was that "political faith" rather than belief was at work. Possibly because he did not wish to leave Senior with this impression, Tocqueville hastened to gratuitously add that many men of intelligence were devout Catholics.[65]

Despite, or perhaps because of, their confusion and ambiguity, these comments are significant. They suggest that Tocqueville was far too sanguine about religious developments during the Second Republic. Because of his assumption of the normality of belief, he supposed that the new sympathy towards the Church would lead to a sincere return to religion, a return that was not merely a reflection of fear of revolution and of socialism. The point is not simply that Tocqueville found it repugnant to explain the influence of Catholicism in terms of the kind of crass "political faith" exemplified by Thiers' sudden rapprochement with the Church, but that his preconceptions allowed him to dismiss this typical attitude as unnatural.* And so he underestimated the extent to which the apparent accommodation between the Church and the Second Republic was really an alliance between the Church and the property-holding classes in the interests of social order. The participants in this alliance might readily dispense with the Republic and with liberty, if their aims could best be served otherwise. Very shortly this did occur, and Napoleonic rule became a reality. Tocqueville then began to inveigh against both the hypocrisy of a "political faith" and the willingness of the Church to sanction the new regime. Removed from political power, and indeed from political participation, by the coup d'état of 1851, he was to assess the relations between religion and politics with far more acuteness than had been possible during the Second Republic. In short, political loss was to be turned to theoretical gain.

*In one of his letters of this period Tocqueville wrote that a serious and lasting return to religion could only come about as a result of each individual realizing "l'indispensable nécessité des croyances." His aim at this point was however not to contrast real faith with "political faith," but to warn against government action as a means of fostering religious revival. See Tocqueville to Corcelle, Sept. 13, 1851, *Oeuvres* (B), VI, pp. 179–182.

Notes

1. Tudesq, op. cit., vol. 2, pp. 1096, 1227; Rémusat, op. cit., vol. 4, pp. 402-403.

2. Tocqueville, "Profession de foi," March 19, 1848. In *Assemblée constituante, élections, la Manche-1848.*

3. Tocqueville, "Discours prononcé à l'Assemblée constituante dans la discussion du projet de constitution sur la question du droit au travail," Sept. 12, 1848, in *Oeuvres* (B), IX, pp. 540-546.

4. Ibid., pp. 551-552.

5. On the assistance measures taken by the Cavaignac government during this period see Frederick A. de Luna, *The French Republic under Cavaignac, 1848* (Princeton, 1969), pp. 271-274, and Dreyfus, op. cit., pp. 73-95.

6. On the reform efforts of the Cavaignac government, and social Catholic advocacy of them, see de Luna, op. cit., ch. 10-12; Dreyfus, op. cit., ch. 3-7; Duroselle, op. cit., pp. 434-474.

7. *Compte rendu des séances de l'Assemblée nationale* (Paris, 1849-50), Dec. 11, 1848, vol. 6, p. 219.

8. Ibid., July 5, 1848, vol. 2, p. 358.

9. de Luna, op. cit., pp. 294-295.

10. *Compte rendu,* Nov. 15, 1848, vol. 5, pp. 570-581.

11. Conversation with Nassau William Senior, Feb. 4, 1851, in *Correspondence and Conversations of Alexis de Tocqueville with Nassau William Senior from 1834 to 1859* (London, 1872), vol. 1, pp. 204-205.

12. Drescher (*Dilemmas,* pp. 230-231) makes substantially the same point.

13. Cited in Maxime du Camp, *Souvenirs de l'année 1848* (Paris, 1876), pp. 112-113.

14. *Compte rendu,* July 5, 1848, vol. 2, pp. 368-369. The best account of this episode is in de Luna, op. cit., pp. 193-199; see also Louis Girard, *La IIe République* (Paris, 1968), pp. 151-152.

15. Tocqueville to Beaumont, Aug. 4, 1839, *Oeuvres* (M), Tome VIII (op. cit.), vol. 1, p. 370; Tocqueville to Beaumont, Sept. 3, 1848, Sept. 24, 1848, *Oeuvres* (M), Tome VIII (op. cit.), vol. 2, pp. 39, 52.

16. For the material in this paragraph see the following: Alfred de Falloux, *Mémoires d'un royaliste* (Paris, 1925), vol. 2, pp. 3-10; Edouard Lecanuet, *Montalembert* (Paris, 1895-1902), vol. 2, pp. 416-419; Henri Michel, *La loi Falloux* (Paris, 1906), pp. 10-22.

17. Falloux, op. cit., p. 32.

18. Rémusat, op. cit., pp. 149-151, discusses Corcelle's background and personality with much acuteness. Alan B. Spitzer, in *Old Hatreds and Young Hopes. The French Carbonari against the Bourbon Restoration* (Cambridge, Mass., 1971), p. 305, includes both Corcelle and his father among the known Carbonarists active during the Restoration. In Michel's judgment, Corcelle, despite his liberal connections, was identified with the Catholic position on teaching and therefore was not a neutral member of the commission. (Michel, op. cit., pp. 33, 98, 173.)

19. Girard, op. cit., pp. 191-194.

20. For Tocqueville's description of the political situation, and of the

formation of the new ministry see Tocqueville, *Souvenirs,* in *Oeuvres* (M), Tome XII, pp. 197–207. This should be compared with the accounts in Odilon Barrot, *Mémoires posthumes* (Paris, 1875–76), vol. 3, pp. 282–283, and Falloux, op. cit., p. 78. Charles Alméras, *Odilon Barrot* (Paris, 1950), pp. 274–276, and Girard, op. cit., pp. 187–194, are also useful.

21. *Souvenirs,* p. 222.

22. See Paul Gerbod, *La condition universitaire en France au XIXe siècle* (Paris, 1965), pp. 228–229, note.

23. For a summary of the *projet* as it emerged from the commission see Michel, op. cit., pp. 162–171.

24. Conversation with Senior, May 26, 1848, *Correspondence and Conversations,* vol. 1, p. 50; Rémusat, op. cit., p. 281.

25. Procès-Verbaux du Comité de Constitution de 1848 (Archives nationales, C 9I8), June 9, 1848, discussion of article 123 of draft constitution.

26. See Barrot, op. cit., vol. 4, p. 12; Alméras, op. cit., p. 225; Paul Bastid, *Doctrines et institutions politiques de la seconde république* (Paris, 1945), vol. 1, pp. 269–270.

27. The divergence of opinion among Catholics is described by John K. Huckaby, "Roman Catholic Reaction to the Falloux Law," *French Historical Studies,* IV (Fall 1965), pp. 203–213. A somewhat different interpretation is put forward by Anita Rasi May, "The Falloux Law, the Catholic Press, and the Bishops: Crisis of Authority in the French Church," *French Historical Studies,* VIII (Spring 1973), pp. 77–94. On the response to the Falloux bill during the summer of 1849 see Michel, op. cit., pp. 242–243.

28. *Compte rendu,* Nov. 7, 1849, vol. 3, p. 359.

29. For a full account of this episode see Michel, op. cit., pp. 283–327.

30. *Compte rendu,* Jan. 11, 1850, vol. 4, p. 632; on the ratification of the Parieu bill see Michel, op. cit., pp. 348–366.

31. *Compte rendu,* Feb. 21, 1850, vol. 6, p. 23.

32. Ibid., Feb. 23, 1850, vol. 6, p. 74; on the Bourzat amendment see Michel, op. cit., pp. 416–424.

33. *Compte rendu,* Feb. 26, 1850, vol. 6, p. 121.

34. Ibid., March 15, 1850, vol. 6, pp. 416–417.

35. Barrot, op. cit., pp. 12–14.

36. The most detailed and comprehensive account of the effects of the Falloux law during the Second Empire is to be found in the recent essay by Robert Anderson, "The Conflict in Education. Catholic Secondary Schools (1850–1870): A Reappraisal," in Theodore Zeldin, ed., *Conflicts in French Society* (London, 1970), pp. 51–93. See also Dansette, op. cit., pp. 268–271, and Girard, op. cit., pp. 210–211.

37. For a good brief account of these events see de Luna, op. cit., pp. 359–363.

38. Tocqueville to Beaumont, Dec. 1 and Dec. 3, 1848, *Oeuvres* (M), Tome VIII, vol. 2, pp. 105, 108, 114; Conversation with Senior, Feb. 17, 1851, *Correspondence and Conversations,* vol. 1, pp. 236, 238.

39. Lecanuet, op. cit., pp. 418–419; F. A. Simpson, *Louis Napoleon and the Recovery of France* (London, 1951), pp. 56–57.

40. Falloux, op. cit., p. 53.

41. Alméras, op. cit., pp. 259–262; Simpson, op. cit., pp. 62–68.

42. Girard, op. cit., p. 186; Simpson, op. cit., pp. 69–70.

43. Falloux, op. cit., p. 80.

44. *Souvenirs*, pp. 213, 215–216.

45. Ibid., pp. 242–243.

46. Tocqueville to Reeve, July 19, 1849, *Oeuvres* (M), Tome VI (op. cit.), pp. 105–107; Tocqueville to Corcelle, Aug. 4, 1849, in Camille Callier, *Lettres du Col. Callier,* ed. by A. B. Duff and M. Degros (Paris, 1950), p. 180; Tocqueville, speech to Assembly of Aug. 6, 1849, in *Moniteur Universel,* Aug. 7, 1849, p. 2608; Conversation with Senior, Feb. 17, 1851, *Correspondence and Conversations,* vol. 1, p. 234.

47. Dansette, op. cit., pp. 276–277; Duroselle, op. cit., pp. 374–383.

48. Frédéric Arnaud (de l'Ariège), speech to the Assembly of Aug. 6, 1849, in *Moniteur Universel,* Aug. 7, 1849, p. 2607.

49. *Compte rendu,* Aug. 6, 1849, vol. 2, p. 257.

50. Tocqueville to Corcelle, Aug. 28, 1856, cited in Eugène d'Eichthal, *Alexis de Tocqueville et la Démocratie libérale* (Paris, 1897), p. 215.

51. *Compte rendu,* Aug. 6, 1849, vol. 2, pp. 259–260.

52. Tocqueville to Corcelle, Aug. 4, 1849, in Callier, op. cit., p. 181; Tocqueville, speech to the Assembly of Oct. 18, 1849, in Tocqueville, *Recollections* (New York, 1959), pp. 315, 321–322; Maurice Degros, "Les 'Souvenirs,' Tocqueville et la question romaine," in *Alexis de Tocqueville: Livre du centenaire, 1859–1959,* pp. 164–170; Edward T. Gargan, *Alexis de Tocqueville: The Critical Years, 1848–1851* (Washington, 1955), pp. 149–167. Falloux, whose aim was quite simply Papal restoration, admitted that Tocqueville would not have publicly affirmed acceptance of the temporal power had he not also been able to press for reform. See Falloux, op. cit., pp. 118–119.

53. Tocqueville to Callier, Aug. 9, 1849, in Callier, op. cit., pp. 177–178; Degros, op. cit., pp. 163–164; Emile Bourgeois and Emile Clermont, *Rome et Napoléon III* (Paris, 1907), p. 192.

54. Gobineau to Tocqueville, Aug. 31, 1849, Tocqueville to Corcelle, Sept. 2, 1849, *Oeuvres* (M), Tome IX (op. cit.), p. 85 and note; Tocqueville to Corcelle, Aug. 4 and Aug. 19, 1849, in Callier, op. cit., pp. 179–184; Degros, op. cit., p. 166; Gargan, op. cit., p. 160.

55. Roger Aubert, *Le Pontificat de Pie IX* (Paris, 1952), p. 38; E. E.Y. Hales, *Pio Nono* (New York, 1954), pp. 152–153.

56. Tocqueville to Beaumont, Oct. 12, Sept. 27, Oct. 5, Oct. 12, Oct. 20, Dec. 5, 1849, *Oeuvres* (M), Tome VIII (op. cit.), vol. 2, pp. 200, 423, 426–427, 438, 449, 259–260; Degros, op. cit., pp. 166–168. These sources also reveal the extent to which Corcelle's complaisance toward the Papal court was a source of embarrassment to Tocqueville throughout the negotiations.

57. Tocqueville, speech to the Assembly of Oct. 18, 1849, in *Recollections,* pp. 317–319, 321–323.

58. Simpson, op. cit., p. 82.

59. Conversation with Senior, Feb. 17, 1851, *Correspondence and Conversations,* vol. 1, pp. 239–240.

60. Ibid., p. 234.

61. Ibid., May 26, 1848, March 8, 1849, pp. 50, 56.

62. *Souvenirs,* pp. 94, 99, 121–122. The older histories of the Second Republic put forward the same interpretation. See Pierre de la Gorce, *Histoire de la seconde République française* (Paris, 1919), vol. 1, pp. 120-122, and Charles Seignobos, *La Révolution de 1848—le second empire* (Paris, 1921), p. 21. Recent regional studies have however shown that anticlericalism accompanied the February Revolution. See Christianne Marcilhacy, *Le diocèse d'Orléans au milieu du XIXe siècle* (Paris, 1964), p. 290; Roger Magraw, "The Conflict in the Villages. Popular Anticlericalism in the Isère (1852–1870)," in Zeldin, op. cit., pp. 169–227; Philippe Vigier, *La Seconde République dans la région Alpine* (Paris, 1963), vol. 1, pp. 203–204.

63. *Souvenirs,* pp. 121–122; Conversation with Senior, Aug. 18, 1850, *Correspondence and Conversations,* vol. 1, p. 106; Tocqueville to Corcelle, Sept. 13, 1851, *Oeuvres* (B), VI, pp. 179–182. Similar evaluations are to be found in Dansette, op. cit., pp. 281–283, Thureau-Dangin, op. cit., pp. 479–483, and Tudesq, op. cit., vol. 2, pp. 1234–1235.

64. Conversation with Senior, Aug. 18, 1850, *Correspondence and Conversations,* Vol. 1, p. 107.

65. Ibid.

Chapter V

The Roots of Present Discontents: The Church During the Old Regime and the Second Empire

Throughout 1850 and 1851 there were indications that the heir of the Napoleonic legend would not docilely resign the presidency at the end of his term of office. The one means of averting an illegal seizure of power appeared to be by revising the constitution to permit the reelection of the president. Tocqueville favored this expedient, which would at least temporarily preserve the constitutional structure of the Second Republic, but in July 1851 the Assembly rejected the proposed revision.[1] On December 2 the long-awaited blow fell: the Assembly was dissolved and the draft of a new constitution promulgated. The coup d'état had been well planned in its inception and its execution, and it met with little opposition from either the Assembly or the Parisian workers.[2] As for the Church, neither clergy nor influential laymen raised their voices in protest. Montalembert called for the victory of the Prince–President in the forthcoming plebiscite, arguing that only then would the nation be secure against the menace of socialism.[3] Louis Napoleon's presentation of himself as the saviour of France from anarchy, together with his outright courtship of the clergy, combined to give him the support of the vast majority of Catholics. Of all the Catholic leaders only Lacordaire and the Bishop of Orleans, Dupanloup, were unequivocal in their dislike of the new regime, but it was their silence amid the chorus of acclaim that revealed their feelings.[4]

The plebiscite resulted in a resounding victory for Louis Napoleon, a victory not to be divorced from official pressure, but one in which memories of June 1848 and recent provincial uprisings undoubtedly played a more important part. The assent of the nation to the coup d'état having been secured, the organization of the government was now taken in hand. The promised constitution was drawn up, and from it emerged a system which, under some faint pretence of democratic government, allowed complete political power to Louis Napoleon. The lower chamber—the Corps Législatif—was indeed elected by universal manhood suffrage, but because of the numerous restrictions constitutionally placed upon it, the new body was far from being a strong and vocal bulwark of constitutional government.[5] Until the end of March 1852, when the government set up by the new constitution came into existence, Louis Napoleon governed through decrees, and the laws promulgated at this time were indicative of the policies to be pursued throughout the period of the Second Empire. Economic measures were taken that laid a basis for the prosperity of the nation, while these same months also saw arrests, deportations, and censorship.[6] The pattern was clear: material well-being was to be promoted, but political liberty was to be discouraged and repressed.

Tocqueville's active involvement in French politics was brought to an abrupt end by the coup d'état. He refused to associate himself in any way with a regime that he believed had destroyed free and constitutional government, and he retired from public life. In a private letter written two months after the coup d'état he protested vehemently against the argument that adherence to the regime could be justified on the grounds that Louis Napoleon was serving the cause of public morality, religion, and authority. Did perjury, deception, and violence serve the cause of morality, he asked? Was the violation of the law and the punishment of those who remained loyal to their oaths in the public good? Again, did the arbitrary arrests and deportations that were taking place indicate respect for law?[7] He was both saddened and angered by the general willingness to accept such a government, and was unable to delude himself with the hope that it would be more than a transitory phenomenon. On the contrary, the regime appeared to be firmly entrenched, since it was based upon the over-whelming desire to have done with political agitation and the "phantom of socialism," and to return to the serious business of money-making.[8] Napoleonic rule would endure until the French were ready to rouse themselves from their torpor and again assume the responsibility of free institutions. Until that day arrived, Tocqueville considered abstention from politics to be obligatory. This remained his position until his death in 1859.[9]

Tocqueville's disgust with French political life during the fifties was multiplied tenfold as he witnessed, not merely the acceptance, but the adulation of the regime by Catholic clergy and laity. Before the coup d'état, he had expressed anxiety about the willingness of influential Catholics to use the temporal power as a means of buttressing the religious revival.[10] By 1852 there could be no doubt that a new alliance between Church and state was being forged.[11] Religion, Tocqueville wrote, has made itself the accomplice of the regime, has readily cast off its supposed devotion to liberty, and has become the shameless sycophant of Louis Napoleon.[12] His letters throughout the fifties, and especially those to Corcelle, record his "sadness, almost despair" regarding the obsequious conduct of the clergy.[13] On one occasion he took to task a Bishop who had described Louis Napoleon in a pastoral letter as "the Envoy of the Most High, the Chosen One, the Minister of divine wisdom." Is it wise, he asked, for the Church to consecrate the regime in this way, to acclaim it "in the name of God"? During the First Empire and the Restoration, the Church acted in similar fashion, and the results were not fortunate for religion. After this pointed warning, Tocqueville underlined the fact that many in France could not accept the existing government because if its immoral acts. These men experienced "a painful uneasiness in the depths of their souls, and a kind of disturbance of their faith, in hearing the most respected authorities excuse such acts in the name of eternal morality."[14]

But Tocqueville's most scathing remarks were reserved for those displays of self-conscious piety that characterized both official circles and public opinion during the Second Empire.[15] He made no secret of his conviction that the prevalent respect for religion did not mean a genuine revival of religious faith. Again and again he spoke scornfully of "nos dévots," of "a kind of religious affectation," of the "semblance" of religious devotion in France.[16] At one point he admitted to Gobineau that if he could not mention the "dévots" without irritation it was because of those who are capable of violent and evil actions, while speaking piously of their "holy religion."[17] His disdain for the religious hypocrisy of the Second Empire had a more important effect than that of rendering Tocqueville caustic: he became extremely sensitive to the distinction between sincere religious faith and outward observance.[18] The truth of Senior's remark that "political faith" was compatible with "general unbelief" now became apparent. For whatever might be the normality of religious belief in theory,

83

it was sham religiosity and willingness to use religion as a vehicle of social and political stability that flourished during the Second Empire. Tocqueville now explicitly distinguished between real faith and the counterfeit coin of "political faith," and recoiled from the latter with disgust. He had always believed that the social efficacy of religion could only make itself felt as a result of sincere religious faith; not until the fifties did he realize that it was possible to regard religion, not as an inherent feeling or need, but solely as an investment in social order.

Not all Catholics were ready to abandon liberal institutions and accept the alliance between the Church and the Second Empire. The new liberal Catholic movement that came into being in the 1850s was composed of both clergy and laity who disapproved of the identification of Catholic interests with the regime. They insisted that liberty of conscience and liberty in the political sphere should be the aim of French Catholicism. By January of 1852 Montalembert had become disillusioned with Louis Napoleon, and he soon became the most articulate spokesman of the movement, using every occasion to attack the government by means of his pen and oratorical talents.[19] But Montalembert, as well as Falloux, Lacordaire, Prince Albert de Broglie, and Dupanloup, all of whom joined him in opposition, were "generals without troops."[20] The pervasive lack of interest in political questions, the acquiescence of the nation to the coup d'état and to the establishment of the Empire in the next year, partially account for the lack of influence of the liberal Catholics. Both political inertia and the belief that Louis Napoleon was the protector of the Church were capitalized upon by Louis Veuillot. This vocal propagandist of authoritarianism filled the pages of L'Univers with the most violent attacks against the liberal Catholics, and indeed against all opponents of the divinely ordained emperor of the French. Unhappily, it was Veuillot and the Univers that commanded the widest audience among French Catholics. His hold upon the lower clergy was almost complete, and he was armed with the approbation of Pius IX. It was left to the liberal Catholics, together with the legitimists and Orleanists, to carry on their warfare against the regime in the limited circles of the Académie française and the Parisian salons.[21]

During this period the liberal Catholics were also engaged in fighting a courageous, though ultimately fruitless, battle against the authoritarian Ultramontanism of Veuillot. Until the Second Empire, Ultramontanism in France had been associated with liberal Catholicism, with the attempt to root out the Gallican theory of the submission of the Church to the state. By

84

the fifties, however, Ultramontanism was being transformed into what Montalembert called "a school of servitude," in which "those basely servile in temporal affairs and insolently oppressive in spiritual affairs were endeavoring to establish an execrable solidarity between Ultramontanism and despotism."[22] This was an accurate description of the situation throughout Europe, caused in large part by the fact that after his return from exile Pius IX encouraged both political reaction and ecclesiastical centralization. The restoration of the Catholic hierarchy in England in 1850, the proclamation of the dogma of the Immaculate Conception in 1854, the Concordat with Austria in 1855—these were the milestones upon the road to Papal Infallibility, that final victory reached by Ultramontanism in 1870.[23]

Tocqueville was aware of the new aggressive stance of Ultramontanism, but he did not consider it an evil commensurate with that of the submission of the French Catholic Church to Louis Napoleon. He admitted to Senior that the restoration of an English hierarchy had been unwise, since the result was "fear and resentment," and the consequent decline of Papal influence in England.[24] He did not, however, direct his attention to the implications of Pius IX's action, or to the reasons why it evoked cries of "Papal Aggression," and was unpopular even among English Catholics. By 1856 Tocqueville had evidently given more thought to the question of Papal policies, but his conclusions indicate that he was far more willing to criticize the Pope as temporal prince than as head of the Church. He had come to think that the Papacy was "more or less in opposition to the political tendencies of the times," and that it was the Pope's position as temporal ruler that caused his political conservatism.[25] Hence, Tocqueville abandoned the position that he had held in 1849 and decided that the Papal States were a bane to the Church.

Yet, in commenting upon an article written by Henry Reeve on the subject of the Austrian Concordat, he tended to minimize the menace posed by increased Papal power over the Church itself. While recognizing the growth of Ultramontanism, he insisted that it was a spontaneous movement, reflecting the Catholic revival throughout Europe rather than the influence of Pius IX.[26] He went on to discuss a question that he considered of the first importance; namely, the respective risks posed to the freedom of the Church by both Ultramontanism and Gallicanism. The servitude of the Church does result, he admitted to Reeve, when the Pope functions as an absolute monarch, unrestrained by the rights of the clergy. This is indeed the present tendency, and Reeve is correct in pointing out

85

the dangers of Ultramontanism. Nevertheless, the other form of servitude to which the Church can be subjected, that of becoming an instrument of the state, is far worse. Nothing, Tocqueville asserted, is more "detestable" than the latter. Freedom from the hegemony of Rome may only mean, as in the case of Bossuet, submission of the Church to the will of a ruler, with the clergy reduced to providing a religious sanction for absolutism. In conclusion, Tocqueville stated frankly that if he were forced to choose between the two forms of servitude, he preferred "the subjection of the Church to its spiritual head, and in this sense the exaggerated separation of the two powers, rather than the union of the two in the hands of a temporal despot."[27]

Because of his single-minded concern with the dangers of clerical subservience to the temporal power, Tocqueville never came to grips with the implications of the new Ultramontanism. He did not realize, for example, that the same thirst for absolutism gave rise to Veuillot's panegyrics of Louis Napoleon and to his call for Papal supremacy in religious affairs. And Veuillot was merely the leading French proponent of the ideas held by the new Ultramontanes throughout Catholic Europe. Devoted to Papal centralization, they were also uncompromising enemies of what was later to be summed up in the *Syllabus of Errors* as "recent civilization."[28] As a result, Montalembert and his associates, to whom Ultramontanism had meant the freedom of the Church from the state, began to draw away from their position, refusing to be associated with the "idolatry of the temporal and of the spiritual power" of Veuillot and his adherents.[29] Nor could an acute onlooker dismiss the extremism of French Ultramontanism as a reflection of the egregious personality of Veuillot. It was the ideas of *L'Univers* that were applauded at Rome, and there was no doubt that in countenancing Veuillot's attack on members of the episcopate as well as on the liberals, Pius IX was encouraging the growth of the new, authoritarian Ultramontanism.[30] The promulgation of the *Syllabus of Errors* and the acceptance of the doctrine of Papal Infallibility occurred after Tocqueville's death. Neither did he live to see the Pope more-or-less explicitly single out Veuillot, Cardinal Manning, and Donoso Cortes, the advocates of political and religious absolutism, as the champions of the Church. Nevertheless, it is surprising that the example of Veuillot did not alert so astute an observer as Tocqueville to the fact that the issue was not merely one of subjecting the Church to its spiritual chief, but of the acceptance by the Vatican of authoritarianism in religious and political life.

To some extent, his rather sanguine attitude followed from his view of Ultramontanism as an exaggerated separation between Church and state, and therefore to be feared less than the submission of religion to the secular power. And yet it might have been expected that this purely theoretical judgment would recede in importance when confronted with the brute fact of the frankly authoritarian tendencies of Ultramontanism. But because his attitude towards the protagonists in the quarrel between liberal Catholicism and Ultramontanism was determined solely by the touchstone of opposition to Louis Napoleon, this did not occur. Although Tocqueville knew the liberal Catholics, warmly praised their speeches and writings when these were directed against the government, and with varying degrees of enthusiasm supported the entrance of Montalembert, Falloux, Dupanloup, and Broglie into the *Académie française*, he never really trusted them. This is shown most clearly in the opinions he expressed about Montalembert, whom he never forgave for having briefly supported Louis Napoleon after the coup d'état. Years after Montalembert had become one of the most steadfast opponents of the regime, Tocqueville interpreted the Catholic leader's political behavior in the most disparaging terms. At the time of the coup d'état, he explained to Senior, Montalembert thought that Louis Napoleon was Ultramontane, and had therefore been as servile as the *Univers* was at present. Despite his change of position, there is only a nuance rather than a fundamental divergence between Montalembert and his "great enemy," the *Univers*.[31] The inference is plain: Tocqueville evidently believed that Montalembert's opposition to the regime was based, not on principle, but on Louis Napoleon's refusal to favor the Church to the extent that the Catholic leader desired. Hence, the conclusion that there was no real difference between the views of Montalembert and those of Veuillot, since both were concerned only with the interests of the Church. Many of Tocqueville's references to both Montalembert and Falloux during these years have the same slighting, critical tone. This stemmed from his belief that the quality of their opposition to Louis Napoleon left something to be desired, since it was based on expediency rather than on principle.[32]

This moral rigor, so similar to that of Lord Acton's judgments upon Dupanloup and even upon Döllinger, resulted in a skewing of vision.[33] To say that there was no real difference between the positions of Montalembert and of Veuillot, since both men were devoted to the interests of the Church, is to ignore the fact that their conception of those interests was radically different. But Tocqueville's thoroughgoing contempt of French Catholicism for playing the pander to Louis Napoleon rendered him incapable of recognizing what were, in fact, genuine distinctions. He was more prone to cry "a plague on both your houses" than to weigh the reasons for the profound cleavage that the new, authoritarian Ultramontanism had caused. Consequently, his rigorous principles, admirable though they were, resulted not only in injustice to liberal Catholicism itself, but also in failure to measure adequately the threat of Ultramontanism to the very values he esteemed.

When the French political arena ceases to be the cynosure of attention, the tendency to cavil at the excessive rigor of Tocqueville's judgments gives way to admiration. For although the years between 1851 and his death in 1859 were bitter and frustrating to the *homme politique,* he was able to turn personal anguish to the uses of knowledge. Richard Herr's recent book has shown how Tocqueville's response to the Second Empire shaped both the subject matter and the composition of *L'Ancien Régime et la Révolution.*[34] His treatment of such fundamental themes as liberty, democracy, equality, and centralization, which had been hammered out during the writing of the *Démocratie,* had to be recast in order to explain why France had yielded to a new Napoleonic dictatorship. Another basic question that had always preoccupied Tocqueville was that of how various societies succeeded in maintaining a sense of public morality among their citizens. Now, witnessing the alacrity with which French Catholics accepted the Second Empire, he began to scrutinize the relationships between Christianity and citizenship.

One of the most elusive and yet pervasive themes of Tocqueville's thought is what he variously calls "public spirit," "public morality," or "public virtue." For present purposes there is no need to discuss the development of his concept of citizenship, but it is important to understand that he began with the assumption that the basis of public morality had been called into question by the advent of democratization.[35] Love of country and the willingness to sacrifice private interests to the common good had hitherto been the hallmark of public morality. Could these qualities continue to exist despite the egoistic individualism and self-seeking materialism that prevailed in democratic societies?

The example of America had provided an answer to this question, enabling Tocqueville to frame the outlines of a theory of citizenship suited to new social and political conditions. He had decided that although the American republic was not animated by disinterested love of country, there did exist a "patriotism of reflection" based on enlightened self-interest.[36] The ability to recognize one's own interest in the common interest could be stimulated by means of political participation. Only when men have political rights, as they did in the United States, would they become aware of their stake in the affairs of the nation.[37] He had noted with approval how certain American institutions, namely, the jury system and local self-government, fostered that practical political education that makes good citizens. The deleterious effects of individualism and materialism were also minimized through the constant exercise of political rights, particularly in local affairs. At this level, the connection between private and public interest was evident, and the citizen learned that he was tied to the community by bonds of enlightened self-interest.[38] In short, the example of America had taught Tocqueville that it was possible to maintain public morality in a democracy by means of political participation acting upon enlightened self-interest. Religion played a part in this scheme of things only insofar as the pervasive acceptance of the Christian ethic provided a latent system of norms and restraints. There is no indication that Tocqueville's American experience led him to stress the overt use of organized religion as a means of reinforcing citizenship.

In Tocqueville's judgment France during the July Monarchy was the hapless example of a nation that had failed to sustain a feeling of public spirit among its citizens. Both enlightened self-interest and meaningful political participation were lacking, and the evils of individualism and materialism were ubiquitous.[39] As a remedy, Tocqueville called for parliamentary reform; that is, the removal of placemen, as well as extension of the suffrage. The first of these measures would remove the taint of corruption that was poisoning political life. The second might restore to the French a sense of involvement in political affairs. Neither reform was enacted during the lifetime of the July Monarchy. Perhaps out of desperation, Tocqueville even advocated an aggressive foreign policy and the conquest of Algeria as a means of reanimating public morality.[40] There is an indication in the 1843 dialogue with Gobineau that Tocqueville was also, for the first time, considering the relationship between Christianity and citizenship from a point of view different than that suggested by the American experience. He was apparently thinking in terms of Christianity explicitly concerning itself with the duties of citizenship, rather than acting only as a latent regulative principle.[41] He did not stress this point, however, and it remained only a foreshadowing of ideas that were to be developed later, as a response to political conditions far more distressing than those of the July Monarchy.

The Revolution of 1848 had, for one brief moment, promised to cleanse France of corruption and apathy in a tide of political idealism.* These hopes were blighted by the class warfare of the June Days and finally extinguished by the coup d'état. Political apathy, individualism, and a self-seeking materialism flourished more rampantly than ever, exacerbated now by the violence and illegality of the Napoleonic regime. How had this come about? Who was responsible? Was it the fault of those who had grasped power in 1830 or in 1848, or did the French past itself have to be arraigned? In *L'Ancien Régime et la Révolution* Tocqueville attempted to answer these questions. Richard Herr has argued that the central theme of the book is the inability of France to become a liberal democracy because the fiscal and administrative system of the monarchy destroyed public virtue.[42] Certainly, the *Ancien Régime* expresses Tocqueville's conviction that only political rights can preserve public morality in a democratic society. Large sections of the book are devoted to describing the progress of centralization, which destroyed the political rights of the estates and of local and municipal bodies. In contrast, Tocqueville cites the example of the clergy and of the *pays d'état*, which had managed to preserve some political rights. The moral is that public spirit endured insofar as decentralization and political participation continued to exist.[43]

The one new aspect of Tocqueville's discussion of citizenship in the *Ancien Régime* is his emphasis on the role of the clergy in fostering public morality. He attributed the public virtue of the pre-Revolutionary clergy partially to the effects of decentralization, but it was primarily the ownership of landed property that enabled the priests to share the needs and feelings of citizenship. Consequently, it is unwise to deprive the clergy of landed property and substitute a fixed salary, since property ownership is the only tie a priest can have to the country in which he lives. Without family, dependent upon the secular power for his income and the Papacy in matters of conscience, totally indifferent to political matters, he becomes "an excellent member of the Christian community, but otherwise a mediocre citizen."[44] The crucial point that Tocqueville stressed was that lack of public virtue on the part of the clergy, who act as the teacher of youth and arbiter of morals, must result in loss of citizenship throughout the nation.[45] The solution, then, is for the clergy to concern itself with public affairs, so that it can instill public spirit into the nation.

Tocqueville's correspondence illustrates his preoccupation with the

*In the *Souvenirs* (pp. 122–23), Tocqueville noted that the members of the Constituent Assembly were more concerned with the public welfare and less given to calculations of self-interest than their predecessors of the July Monarchy.

entire question of Christianity, the Catholic clergy, and citizenship. He was, for example, forced to explain and defend the ideas he had put forward in the *Ancien Régime* concerning the clergy and public morality to Mme. Swetchine, who frankly expressed her misgivings.* He disagreed with her contention that the clergy should be identified with the nation only in terms of "moral attachment," arguing that because the French clergy emphasizes only private morality, the nation at large has not been taught the duties of citizenship.[46] In the course of defending Catholicism and Christianity against Tocqueville's strictures, Mme. Swetchine observed that he was emphasizing the connection between Christianity and citizenship because of French political conditions. But while the desire to find a means of remedying the prevalent apathy and materialism was understandable, all intrusions of the Church into public affairs were undesirable. The mission of Catholicism is compromised, she explained, when the Church puts itself at the service of any political idea or regime.[47] In his reply Tocqueville vehemently denied that he wanted the clergy either to countenance or to criticize particular political opinions. It is not a question of indoctrinating either royalism or republicanism, but rather of the clergy teaching that men are citizens as well as Christians, that they belong to one of the great collective beings, or nations, that God has formed.[48] With extraordinary passion and eloquence Tocqueville went on to outline those principles that he would have members of the clergy teach:

> I want them to impress upon men's minds that each owes himself first of all to this collective being; that indifference with respect to this collective being is not permissible, still less making of indifference a kind of flabby virtue which enervates some of the noblest instincts we have been given; that each is responsible for what happens to this being, and that each, according to his wisdom, is obligated to work continually for its well-being and to take care that it submit only to beneficial, respectable, and legitimate authority.[49]

He concluded with the forthright assertion that merely to obey the existing authority is not Christian public virtue. The duty of the good Christian (and citizen) is to abate the evils of bad government by any means that his conscience may suggest.[50]

*Sophie Swetchine (1782–1857), a devout Roman Catholic convert of Russian birth, settled in Paris in 1825. From the time of July Monarchy, her salon was a center of liberal Catholic discussion and activity. During the fifties she became one of those few individuals with whom Tocqueville was willing to discuss his personal religious attitudes as well as religious questions in general. The standard biography is that of Alfred de Falloux, *Mme. Swetchine, sa vie et ses oeuvres* (Paris, 1860).

In other letters Tocqueville reiterated the same points: the failure of the French clergy since 1789 either to act as citizens or to teach public morality; the consistent weakness of Christianity with regard to citizenship; and the insistence that unqualified submission to the sovereign power was not required by Christian public morality.[51] There is no doubt that the introduction of these motifs marks a shift in Tocqueville's thinking. Until the fifties the active components in his concept of citizenship had been political participation and enlightened self-interest, with Christianity—defined as the pervasive value system of the West—acting only as the latent source of all morality. During the July Monarchy he had commented upon the shortcomings of Christianity in the area of public morality, but he believed that some improvement was taking place. The advent of Napoleonic rule was new and bitter proof of the extent of Christianity's failure to encourage citizenship. And yet, even while castigating the clergy and the Church, he insisted more vehemently than ever before on their potential role in fostering public morality. This was not paradox but a simple lack of alternatives. The French had not learned to think in terms of enlightened self-interest, and participation in politics had been snuffed out. Hence, religion as an organized institution was called upon: the Catholic clergy, representatives of the prevalent form of Christianity in France, must consciously set about the task of reanimating public spirit. The overt use of organized religion thus became a means towards the end of restoring a sense of citizenship, a means that became necessary when it appeared that other expedients had failed.

Tocqueville never considered whether his demand that the clergy become involved in political affairs and teach public morality was at all feasible in nineteenth-century France. He envisioned the French clergy as a strong, independent body, bound by ties of feeling and interest to the nation, but nevertheless free of domination by the state. Was this possible in a society in which church–state relations were defined by the Concordat and the Organic Articles? The state was eminently willing to use the moral and organizational strength of the Church for its own purposes, but was not about to encourage the Catholic priesthood to exercise its own judgment in political matters. And the Church itself, not yet prepared to disavow its traditional ideas and claims, was regarded with suspicion by a society that tended to exaggerate the threat of Catholic domination. Only in the twentieth century has the Church been able to exert moral leadership in political and social affairs without arousing distrust. Before this became possible the trauma of separation between Church and state had to be undergone, as well as a slow change in attitudes on the part of both Church and state. Tocqueville was aware that the institutional framework that made the Church dependent upon the state impeded the development of public spirit among the clergy. In the *Ancien Régime* he stated explicitly that the effect of substituting clerical salaries for the ownership of landed property was to deprive the nation of an independent clergy, and render its members subservient both to the Papacy and to the temporal power. But not even in his private correspondence did Tocqueville take the next step and suggest that termination of the Concordat was the essential precondition for a clergy imbued with public morality. He too was a prey to those doubts and hesitations which, by making separation of church and state seem impracticable, prevented the growth of a public-spirited clergy. Nevertheless, he did set forth a view of the public responsibilities of the Church which was to take on reality much later. The twentieth century has provided dramatic evidence of the willingness of French priests to involve themselves in social reform movements, in the Resistance, and in opposition to the conduct of the Algerian War. D. W. Brogan, in explaining Catholic attitudes toward the Algerian War, has spoken of "the acceptance of the idea that a Christian citizen has more duties than and different duties from those that the state defines and demands."[52] This is precisely what Tocqueville would have approved: the willingness of Catholics, clergy and laity alike, to acknowledge that Christian public morality required more than obedience to the existing secular power.

The neglect of public morality on the part of the French clergy was, to Tocqueville, one manifestation of the persistent weakness of Christianity with regard to citizenship. Why then did he continue to maintain that the Gospels were the basis of all morality, public and private? The answer is almost self-evident: he believed that Christianity "ought to be" the basis of all morality. What was at work was that unconscious sleight of hand, observable again and again, which resulted in a weaving together of personal religious attitudes and historical or sociological analysis. His own religious beliefs and commitments were strong enough to lead him to the conclusion that Christianity "ought" to provide the basis of ethics. One consequence of this point of view was that Tocqueville never really analyzed the reasons for the ineffectiveness of Christianity in the sphere of public morality, although he himself had raised the problem. Since he was convinced that the Gospels were the basis of all ethics, it followed logically that any inadequacy must be attributed to adventitious circumstances, rather than to Christian teaching itself. Hence, he did not find it necessary to consider whether Christianity was inherently compatible with the duties of citizenship, although this had been a perennial subject of debate from at least the time of St. Augustine. His reading of Machiavelli and Rousseau must have acquainted him with some of the classical arguments put forward by those who contended that Christianity was not conducive to good citizenship. And even Montesquieu, whose opinions Tocqueville pondered with respect, had been ambiguous on the subject.[53] But for Tocqueville, this was not a matter open to speculation: his early education, his own convictions, and that era harrowed by revolutions in which he lived prompted him to see in Christianity the source of all morality. And French political conditions during the fifties served to reinforce this turn of mind.

Tocqueville's discussion of the revolutionaries of 1789 in the *Ancien Régime* explicitly revealed his belief that no secular ethic could provide a satisfactory basis for public morality. The revolutionary leaders were totally irreligious, he explained, but they had a profound faith in the goodness and perfectibility of man and in the possibility of transforming and regenerating society. The ideals and theories of the Enlightenment became a religion for them, a religion that shared the quality of universality with the religious revolutions of the past. Both approached the large questions of human nature and destiny without reference to the particular facts of race, class, or history. Precisely because of their universal appeal, the ideas of the French Revolution were able to arouse an enthusiasm unprecedented by any previous political revolution. Like earlier religious upheavals, the French Revolution wished to proselytize in the name of its gospel, and succeeded in overrunning all of Europe with its soldiers, apostles, and martyrs.[54]

Although he was lavish in his praise of the heroism, disinterestedness, and public spirit that the secular ideals of the Enlightenment had been able to inspire, Tocqueville nevertheless concluded that the irreligion of the revolutionaries caused great harm. Once the traditional principles in both politics and religion were destroyed, all accepted rules of behavior vanished, and people no longer knew how to govern themselves. Complete loss of stability gave rise to a group of audacious and unscrupulous men who feared no excess or innovation. And this race of revolutionaries is still alive, still a threat to all societies in which it exists. Because of its propensity towards extreme egalitarianism, France was especially vulnerable to the attacks of those who called for further upheaval and the destruction of the remaining barriers of social and economic inequality.[55] A secular ethic, then, even though it might spark the most selfless and passionate idealism, was thoroughly undesirable in France.

In terms of Tocqueville's own beliefs, this position is logical enough. He had, after all, always insisted that the norms and restrictions imposed by religion were necessary in any society, and particularly in a democratic society. But in terms of nineteenth-century France, his refusal to consider any surrogate for Christianity is, if not remarkable, at least notable. For while there was widespread agreement that France was in need of some system of belief that could provide the basis for public as well as private values, the overt statement of the problem usually implied the conviction that Roman Catholicism could no longer fulfill this role.[56] Even Victor Cousin's very moderate attempt at a *morale laïque*, with all its willingness to live at peace with Christianity, did assume that it was necessary to imbue French youth with a common set of philosophical principles in the interests of national unity and stability.[57] Despite Cousin's recognition of the usefulness of the Christian moral code and his willingness to incorporate it into his "official philosophy," Tocqueville, who knew Cousin, never evinced the slightest interest in the latter's ideas. Although Tocqueville frequently spoke of the Christian ethic in pragmatic terms, he believed this ethic to be bound to the Christian religion, at least in some minimal sense. For example, he described the "new religion" that animated the men of 1789 as an "imperfect religion," because it was "without God, without creed and without an afterlife."[58] Fundamentally, the very concept of a secular religion was alien to Tocqueville, since any such concept must, by definition, deny that ethical systems properly have their origins in a "superempirical, transcendent reality."[59] His emphasis on the pernicious social consequences of the quasi-religious ideology of 1789 is a reflection of this attitude, and it explains his somewhat schematic presentation of an important and complicated subject.

Notwithstanding the increased emphasis on the role of religion in promoting public morality to be found in Tocqueville's writings during the fifties, it would be misleading to suggest that there was a radical change in his concept of citizenship. He had always implicitly assumed that Christianity, the religion of the West, was the fount of all morality. From the first he had situated the issue of citizenship within the context of democratization, which meant that those methods through which public morality had been maintained in the past no longer sufficed. The problem then became one of how to imbue large numbers of people with public spirit, using whatever ideological or institutional devices gave promise of success. Hence, great flexibility with respect to means was built into

Tocqueville's concept of citizenship. He had refused to be "scandalized," as Elie Halévy aptly remarked, by the significant role played by enlightened self-interest in sustaining public morality in America.[60] There is ample evidence in the *Ancien Régime* that Tocqueville persisted in the opinion that political participation could be of crucial importance in imparting a sense of citizenship. If circumstances rendered any one of these means ineffectual, he was ready to consider and advocate possible substitutes. What occurred in the fifties was therefore only a shift of focus, an attempt to find in organized Christianity an alternate method of attaining the same goal. In Tocqueville's writings of this period there is an almost frantic casting about for new strategies, new ways of arousing France from the apathy that signalized the decay of public spirit.

To turn to Christianity at the very moment when the French Catholic Church seemed least capable of furthering his own view of citizenship was also an affirmation and a challenge. As against the brutal fact that subservience to an authoritarian state was the sum total of public virtue displayed by most of the French clergy, Tocqueville insisted that obedience was due only to legitimate authority. And because political freedom and constitutional government were his criteria of legitimacy, the concept of civic obligation that he wished the clergy to impart was a direct challenge to the political attitudes of the main body of French Catholicism. In calling upon the clergy to accept his view of the duties imposed by public morality, Tocqueville was reaffirming his lifelong belief that religion must ally itself with liberty.

The defection of the majority of Catholic lay and clerical leaders to the Second Empire forced him to recognize how deeply rooted were the inadequacies of the Church in the public sphere; he searched back into the French past to discover the reasons for these shortcomings. The result was a more realistic and less sanguine appraisal of the obstacles to reconciliation between liberal ideas and French Catholicism than he had been able to formulate during the July Monarchy or the Second Republic. No longer was it possible to nourish the illusion that, despite setbacks, France was becoming a nation in which liberty and religion would work together to alleviate the harmful effects of democratization. The most that could be said was that the trial was not yet over, the outcome not yet certain. Tocqueville's study of various religions did at least provide him with the assurance that Catholicism, in common with other forms of Christianity, was compatible with both liberalism and democracy. During the bleak years of the Second Empire he was able to cling to this certainty and to retain the hope that France would one day arrive at that union of liberty and religion that other societies had achieved.

Notes

1. The fullest account of Tocqueville's efforts in favor of revision is to be found in Gargan, op. cit., pp. 192–216. See also Tocqueville, "Rapport fait à l'Assemblée législative au nom de la commission chargée d'examiner les propositions relatives à la révision de la constitution," July 8, 1851, *Oeuvres* (B), IX, pp. 574–606.

2. On the coup d'état see Adrien Dansette, *Louis Napoléon à la conquête du pouvoir* (Paris, 1961), pp. 343–386; Simpson, op. cit., pp. 120–136; J. M. Thompson, *Louis-Napoleon and the Second Empire* (Oxford, 1954), pp. 116–122. Theodore Zeldin has recently reexamined the question of the extent and sources of opposition to the coup d'état. See Zeldin, *France 1848–1945*, vol. I (Oxford, 1973), pp. 490, 492, 728.

3. Lecanuet, op. cit., vol. 3, pp. 38–39.

4. Dansette, *Louis Napoléon à la conquête du pouvoir*, p. 367; Georges Weill, *Histoire du Catholicisme libéral en France, 1828–1908* (Paris, 1909), pp. 109–112, 117–118.

5. See the *Moniteur Universel* of Jan. 15, 1852, for the text of the constitution. Thompson, op. cit., pp. 127–129, has a convenient summary of its chief provisions.

6. See Simpson, op. cit., pp. 181–184, and Thompson, op. cit., p. 131, for a discussion of Louis Napoleon's activities during these months. Simpson, op. cit., pp. 186–190, has the best account of the repressive measures that were taken.

7. Tocqueville to one of his brothers (unnamed by Redier), Feb. 14, 1852, cited in Redier, op. cit., pp. 229–230.

8. Conversation with Senior, Dec. 23, 1851, *Correspondence and Conversations*, vol. 2, pp. 6–8; Tocqueville to Reeve, Jan. 9, 1852, *Oeuvres* (M), Tome VI (op. cit.), p. 133; Tocqueville to Odilon Barrot, July 3, 1852, *Oeuvres* (B), VII, pp. 287–288; Tocqueville to Lamoricière, Nov. 24, 1852, cited in Redier, op. cit., p. 233.

9. For a judicious appraisal of the historiography on Louis Napoleon and the Second Empire, with which Tocqueville's views may be compared, see Alan B. Spitzer, "The Good Napoleon III," *French Historical Studies*, II, no. 3 (Spring 1962), pp. 308–329. In assessing Tocqueville's views it is important to keep in mind Zeldin's apt remark that "Bonapartism has been the intellectual's nightmare." Zeldin, *France 1848–1945*, I, p. 504.

10. Tocqueville to Corcelle, Sept. 13, 1851, *Oeuvres* (B), VI, pp. 179–182.

11. For a good brief description of what he has called "the honeymoon of the Church and the Empire" see Dansette, *Histoire religieuse de la France contemporaine*, pp. 291–299.

12. Tocqueville to Montalembert, Dec. 1, 1852, *Oeuvres* (B), VII, p. 294.

13. Tocqueville to Corcelle, Sept. 17, 1853, Nov. 15, 1854, *Oeuvres* (B), VI, pp. 228, 280; Tocqueville to Ampère, March 14, 1857, *Oeuvres* (M), Tome XI (op. cit.), p. 371.

14. Tocqueville to Monseigneur_____, March 4, 1858, *Oeuvres* (B), VII, p. 491.

15. On the religiosity of the Second Empire see Dansette, *Histoire religieuse de la France contemporaine,* pp. 291–299, and Thompson, op. cit., pp. 229–232.

16. Tocqueville to Corcelle, Sept. 17, 1853, *Oeuvres* (B), VI, p. 228; Tocqueville to Beaumont, Aug. 28, 1855 and Feb. 27, 1858, *Oeuvres* (M), Tome VIII (op. cit.), vol. 3, pp. 337, 545; Tocqueville to Gobineau, July 30, 1856, *Oeuvres* (M), Tome IX (op. cit.), p. 267; Tocqueville to Ampère, May 25, 1857, *Oeuvres* (M), Tome XI (op. cit.), pp. 380–381.

17. Tocqueville to Gobineau, Jan. 24, 1857, *Oeuvres* (M), Tome IX (op. cit.), p. 278.

18. Tocqueville to Corcelle, Sept. 17, 1853, *Oeuvres* (B), VI, p. 228; Tocqueville to Beaumont, June 17, 1858, *Oeuvres* (M), Tome VIII (op. cit.), vol. 3, p. 577.

19. Dansette, *Histoire religieuse de la France comtemporaine,* pp. 294–299; Lecanuet, op. cit., pp. 44–58; Weill, *Histoire du Catholicisme libéral en France, 1828–1908,* pp. 121–126. For an appraisal of liberal Catholicism that rejects the usual categories of left and right, liberal versus intransigeant Catholics, see J. M. Mayeur, "Catholicisme intransigeant, Catholicisme social, démocratie chrétienne," *Annales,* Mars–Avril 1972, pp. 483–499.

20. Joseph N. Moody, "French Liberal Catholics, 1840–1875," in Evelyn M. Acomb and Marvin L. Brown, Jr., eds., *French Society and Culture Since the Old Regime* (New York, 1966), p. 164. This essay is an excellent account of the liberal Catholic movement, and of the reasons for its failure.

21. Ibid., pp. 162–165. See also Aubert, op. cit., pp. 226–227, 299; Dansette, *Histoire religieuse de la France contemporaine,* pp. 294–299; Weill, op. cit., pp. 110, 122, 126–127.

22. Montalembert to Mgr. Sibour, Sept. 23, 1854, cited in Lecanuet, op. cit., p. 105.

23. For Papal policy during the fifties see Aubert, op. cit., pp. 67–71, 245–310. For a discussion of the ideas of the Ultramontanes and of their liberal Catholic opponents see Gertrude Himmelfarb, *Lord Acton. A Study in Conscience and Politics* (London, 1952), ch. 2, 3, 5.

24. Conversation with Senior, Jan. 25, 1851, *Correspondence and Conversations,* vol. 1, p. 179.

25. Tocqueville to Corcelle, Aug. 28, 1856, cited in Eichthal, op. cit., p. 215.

26. Tocqueville to Reeve, Aug. 7, 1856, *Oeuvres* (M), Tome VI (op. cit.), p. 199.

27. Ibid., p. 200.

28. Aubert, op. cit., pp. 308–309.

29. Montalembert to Mgr. Sibour, Sept. 10, 1853, cited in Lecanuet, op. cit., p. 104.

30. Aubert, op. cit., pp. 298–299; Hales, op. cit., pp. 282–283; Moody, "French Liberal Catholics, 1840–1875," in Acomb and Brown, op. cit., pp. 156, 164.

31. Conversation with Senior, May 2, 1857, *Correspondence and Conversations,* vol. 2, p. 177.

32. Tocqueville to Beaumont, Feb. 1, 1852, March 19, 1855, *Oeuvres* (M), Tome VIII (op. cit.), vol. 3, pp. 20–21, 282; Tocqueville to Ampère, Dec. 27, 1855,

March 14, 1857, *Oeuvres* (M), Tome XI (op. cit.), pp. 305, 369; Conversation with Senior, Apr. 28, 1857, *Correspondence and Conversations*, vol. 2, p. 172.

33. Himmelfarb, op. cit., pp. 147–149, and esp. p. 154.

34. Richard Herr, *Tocqueville and the Old Regime* (Princeton, 1962), pp. 19, 63, 84, 87, 112–114, 118, 127, 130, 134.

35. For a fuller discussion of Tocqueville's view of citizenship see Doris S. Goldstein, "Alexis de Tocqueville's Concept of Citizenship," *Proceedings of the American Philosophical Society*, vol. 108, no. 1 (Feb. 1964), pp. 39–53.

36. Tocqueville, *Voyages en Sicile et aux Etats-Unis*, pp. 234, 286. For evidence of the extent to which Tocqueville had developed this idea before his visit to America see Tocqueville to Charles Stoffels, Apr. 21, 1830, Y. T. Mss, A.VI.

37. *De la démocratie en Amérique*, vol. 1, pp. 245–247. In one of his notebook entries Tocqueville went further, stating that when the exercise of political rights can be extended to all, "les développements de l'esprit public sont presque sans bornes." (Y.T. Mss, C.Vh, Paquet No. 3, Cahier 1, p. 4.)

38. *De la démocratie en Amérique*, vol. 1, pp. 65–67, 109–112, 286–288.

39. There is a plethora of material documenting Tocqueville's somber appraisal of French political life during these years. See especially the following: Tocqueville to Eugène Stoffels, July 16, 1836, Y.T. Mss, C.Ic; Tocqueville to Senior, Aug. 25, 1847, *Correspondence and Conversations*, vol. 1, p. 32; Tocqueville, speeches to the Chamber of Deputies of Jan. 18, 1842, Jan. 28, 1843, Jan. 29, 1848, *Oeuvres* (B(, IX, pp. 374–388, 39, 520–535; *Souvenirs*, pp. 26–30.

40. Tocqueville to John Stuart Mill, Oct. 18, 1840, March 18, 1841, *Oeuvres* (M), Tome VI (op. cit.), pp. 330–331, 335–336; Marcel, op. cit., p. 408; Melvin Richter, "Tocqueville on Algeria," *Review of Politics*, XXV, no. 3 (1963), pp. 381–384.

41. Tocqueville to Gobineau, Sept. 5, 1843, *Oeuvres* (M), Tome IX (op. cit.), pp. 46–47.

42. Herr, op. cit., ch. 7–10.

43. *L'Ancien Régime et la Révolution*, vol. 1, pp. 75, 99–177, 253–261.

44. Ibid., p. 171.

45. Ibid., p. 172.

46. Mme. Swetchine to Tocqueville, Aug. 13, 1856, Tocqueville to Mme. Swetchine, Sept. 10, 1856, in Sophie Swetchine, *Lettres inédites*, ed. by Alfred de Falloux (Paris, 1866), pp. 455, 461.

47. Mme. Swetchine to Tocqueville, Sept. 26, 1856, in Swetchine, op. cit., p. 463.

48. Tocqueville to Mme. Swetchine, Oct. 20, 1856, in Swetchine, op. cit., pp. 466–467.

49. Ibid., p. 467.

50. Ibid., pp. 467–468.

51. Tocqueville to Corcelle, Oct. 23, 1854, Tocqueville to Broglie, July 20, 1856, *Oeuvres* (B), VI, pp. 277–278, 323–324.

52. D. W. Brogan, *Citizenship Today* (Chapel Hill, 1960), pp. 70–71.

53. See Montesquieu's affirmation that Christians can be good citizens in *The Spirit of the Laws*, Bk. XXIV, ch. 6. On the other hand, ch. XXII of the *Considerations on the Greatness and Decline of the Romans* is a critique of the effects of

Christianity on the Eastern Empire. For a recent discussion of the question of Christianity and citizenship see Hannah Arendt, *The Human Condition* (Chicago, 1958).

54. *L'Ancien Régime et la Révolution,* vol. 1, pp. 87–89, 207–208.

55. Ibid., pp. 207–208.

56. See Charlton, op. cit., for a survey of proposed alternatives to Roman Catholicism in nineteenth-century France.

57. See Doris S. Goldstein, "Official Philosophies' in Modern France: The Example of Victor Cousin," *Journal of Social History,* I (Spring 1968), pp. 259-279, for an examination of the aims n's "official philosophy."

58. *L'Ancien Régime et la Révolution,* vol. 1, p. 89.

59. This is the definition of religion set forth by Roland Robertson, *The Sociological Interpretation of Religion* (New York, 1970), p. 47.

60. Elie Halévy, *History of the English People in the Nineteenth Century,* vol. 4, "Victorian Years" (London, 1951), p. 406.

Chapter VI

A Comparative Analysis of Religions, East and West

The use of the comparative method, either explicitly or implicitly, was one of the many ways in which Tocqueville showed himself to be the heir and disciple of Montesquieu.[1] Like his eighteenth-century predecessor, Tocqueville applied this method to the study of religion, ranging from the varieties of Christianity to Islam and Hinduism in his analyses of the social and political consequences of various religious doctrines and institutions. Although he followed Montesquieu in assuming that assessment of the mutual relations among differing religions, societies, and political structures was a significant subject of study, Tocqueville was, in certain respects, more cautious in applying the comparative method to religion. In the eighteenth century, comparative analysis of religious phenomena had the welcome result of dispelling prejudice, but for Tocqueville, living in the aftermath of the French Revolution, irreligion and social chaos appeared to present more imminent perils than did religious intolerance. These perils could only be increased by injudicious pronouncements regarding the suitability—or unsuitability—of particular religions to the emerging democratic societies of the West.

Thus, in both the *Démocratie* and the *Ancien Régime*, major works with a distinct hortatory flavor, Tocqueville was careful not to push his inquiries concerning religious function and dysfunction to the point where they might have a damaging effect upon French *morale*. Specifically, it was in discussions of the social and political consequences of Catholicism and Protestantism that caution became necessary. Montesquieu had called attention to the English ability to unite religion, commerce, and liberty: after the French Revolution this comment took on new significance.[2] In America a republic was established, based on the ideas of the Enlightenment, but also owing much to the traditions and support of the various Protestant sects. In France, on the other hand, the extent of the polarization between the Catholic Church and the Revolution raised the question of whether religion, at least in its French Catholic form, was compatible with the "modern ideas" that were the heritage of 1789.

Tocqueville's account of the relationship of both Catholicism and Protestantism to American institutions reflects his awareness of the sensitivity of the issues involved, and yet it contains substantive contributions to the comparative study of religion. He succeeded in doing justice to the formative role of Puritanism in the development of the American ethos, while maintaining that Catholicism was compatible with democratic theory and practice. In the remarkable chapter of the *Démocratie* dealing with the founding of the New England colonies, he used Montesquieu's suggestion that there is a connection between the form of religious and of political organization to be found in any given state, and he went on to show how democratic and republican attitudes were inherent in Puritanism itself.[3] He was aware that the Puritan union of religious faith and political liberty resulted from the ability to distinguish between religious and political authority, to adhere to fixed rules in the one sphere, while in the political realm establishing "a democracy more perfect than antiquity had dared to dream of."[4] In short, innovation in politics became possible because of the extent to which Puritanism had been able to internalize authority. Although the importance of Tocqueville's scattered remarks should not be exaggerated, they do foreshadow that vast literature, beginning with the work of Max Weber, that explores the psychological ramifications of Puritanism in political and economic life.[5] When, on the other hand, Tocqueville attempted to discuss Catholicism in terms of its inherent affinities with democracy, his arguments were weak and confused, since his didactic concerns blunted rigorous and untrammeled analysis. Nevertheless, he did take the useful step of introducing factors of social class and majority or minority status in order to explain the democratic sentiments of American Catholics. Such considerations tended to be ignored in the polemical atmosphere surrounding discussions of Catholicism and "modern ideas" in nineteenth-century France. To acknowledge the importance of adventitious, nonideational factors was to recognize that the concept of affinities between religious and political doctrines provided too rigid a framework for understanding the interplay of religion, politics, and society. Tocqueville's readiness to move beyond the approach he had inherited from Montesquieu was an advance towards greater flexibility and concreteness in the comparative analysis of religions.

His travels in England and Ireland in 1833 and 1835 gave Tocqueville another opportunity to probe the connections between social structure, political attitudes, and religious affiliation. Moreover, since his impressions never emerged from the privacy of his notebooks, there was no need for caution or edifying pronouncements. In many ways, the conclusions he had reached in America were confirmed, especially those concerning Catholicism. Ireland demonstrated even more strikingly than the United States that the Church was not necessarily hostile to democracy. He noted that the members of the Irish Catholic clergy held extremely liberal and democratic opinions, both in theory and with respect to political conditions in Ireland. They manifested the greatest confidence in the judgment of the people, and shared the desire of their parishioners to rid themselves of English oppression. All believed that the strength of Catholicism lay in its freedom from government ties. What accounted for views so different from those held by most French Catholic priests? The answer was obvious: circumstances. Because the oppressors were Protestant, the Irish Catholic clergy, usually sons of tenant farmers, came to consider themselves as leaders of the people in a cause that was both religious and political.[6] At one point Tocqueville explicitly compared the views of a Catholic priest and of a Protestant clergyman residing in the same Irish village. He came to the intriguing conclusion that in France, the ideas of the former would be taken for those of a Protestant minister and the ideas of the latter would be taken for those of a Catholic priest.[7] Social and political conditions, then, could dispose either religion to democratic or aristocratic sympathies, regardless of its inherent affinities with particular political doctrines.

If, in Ireland, historical and sociological circumstance seemed to determine the political attitudes of both Catholicism and Protestantism, the situation was apparently very different in England. For here it was not a question of religions adjusting to material conditions, but that the varieties of Protestantism attracted followers in terms of social class or political persuasion. Within the confines of Protestantism itself, Tocqueville discovered, there was both the "aristocratic" religion of Anglicanism and the "democratic" religion of the sects. The adherents of the former tended to be among the rich and well-born, while the middle and lower classes belonged to the sects. This was not surprising, since the doctrines of Anglicanism led naturally to monarchical and aristocratic tendencies, and those of the sects to republicanism and democracy.[8] Clearly Tocqueville was again resorting to the idea of affinities between religious and political institutions, with Anglicanism more-or-less comparable to Catholicism. He explicitly made the analogy, pointing out that the Anglican Church was in the same position as the Catholic Church had been in France before 1789: it was rich, it harbored many abuses, and it acted as though it were a political power. The crucial difference was that in England those who were hostile or indifferent to the established Church did not necessarily become irreligious; they joined the sects. He did not discuss Catholicism in England, beyond noting the opinion of various informants that conversions to Catholicism were increasing among those weary of the controversy and agitation characteristic of English sectarianism.[9]

Tocqueville seems to have been of two minds about the social and political implications of that peculiarly English phenomenon, an established Church living side by side with numerous sects. He feared that the existence of an "aristocratic" religion and of a "democratic" religion would increase the polarization of English society. The result might be, not only the eventual destruction of Anglicanism, but the overthrow of the state by the Dissenters, thereby repeating the pattern of 1640. These dire predictions were based upon the assumption that English sectarianism would strengthen (and be strengthened by) the inevitable progress of democratization. This union of religious and political passions might well prove strong enough to sweep away both the established Church and the state. Wide of the mark as these predictions were, they reflect Tocqueville's initial hypothesis that England was the prototype of an aristocratic society under attack. In the course of his 1835 visit he began to revise his views about the stability and resilience of English institutions. Nevertheless, he continued to believe that the animating force of the seventeenth-century English revolutions had been the interlocked religious and political doctrines of the English sects, and that this revolutionary potential still existed.[10]

On the other hand, Tocqueville recognized that despite their latent revolutionary propensities, the sects in nineteenth-century England exercised a restraining influence upon society and politics. For example, many of the political radicals were Dissenters, and the entire tone of English radicalism was free of that hostility to religion and contempt for law and the rights of property that characterized its French counterpart.[11] Here was the positive aspect of having a "democratic" alternative to Anglicanism: political radicalism was itself subject to the norms and restraints imposed by religion. This meant that even if democratization led to thoroughgoing upheaval, its effects would be mitigated. Tocqueville's awareness of the contribution of Dissent to social cohesion in nineteenth-century England is reminiscent of Halévy's magisterial analysis of the influence of the evangelical movement. This is not surprising, for Halévy, like Tocqueville, found "virtue in ideas and religions that encourage gradualism, stability, and social cohesion."[12] Had Tocqueville ever undertaken a study of nineteenth-century England, he probably would have pursued the same line of thought that Halévy was to explore so fruitfully. In so doing, he would have come to understand how the evangelical movement acted as a solvent of revolutionary tendencies and, by forging links among members of different social classes, prevented the polarization that he feared.[13]

As it was, he remained content with the judgment that the pervasiveness of religious belief in England was a protection against the lack of restraint that characterized French radicalism. Particularly during the bitter years of Napoleonic rule, the example of the English ability to unite religion and liberty was a solace and an encouragement. After his third and final visit to England in 1857, Tocqueville commented to Corcelle that he had again had the happiness, too long denied, of seeing a society where harmony existed between religion and the political world, between private and public virtue, between Christianity and liberty. Christians of all denominations consider free institutions necessary to the well-being and morality of society, so that England is spared the "moral monstrosity" of religious men praising despotism, while the irreligious speak in favor of liberty. This is the unnatural situation one sees elsewhere in Europe.[14] Corcelle apparently read an oblique criticism of Catholicism into this letter, for Tocqueville hastened to explain that he was not comparing Protestantism to Catholicism, but rather England to the continent. In England, Catholics as well as Protestants approve of free institutions. Moreover, English Catholics, both clergy and laity, do not separate public from private morality, concerning themselves only with the latter. Tocqueville went on to make this covert reference to the French situation explicit, predicting that the French clergy would come to regret having made a virtue of political indifference. He warned that when men "de nos jours" cease to be involved with political matters, they throw themselves into irreligious and dangerous philosophical theories. By way of evidence he pointed to the apolitical Germans, who were open to revolution in 1848 because the foundations of their society had already been weakened by destructive theories.[15] This is, in fact, a repetition of one of the arguments made in the *Ancien Régime:* those who have no practical experience of political affairs are more likely to spin webs of utopian and unsound theory.

Given the frequency and vehemence of Tocqueville's attacks upon the Church during the fifties, it is easy to understand why Corcelle interpreted his friend's praise of English attitudes as criticism of Catholicism. But even in these private letters Tocqueville disavowed the view that Catholicism was necessarily linked to political authoritarianism, insisting that under proper circumstances Catholicism as well as Protestantism was compatible with free institutions. In the *Ancien Régime* he sought to explain historically how a particular set of conditions in France had brought about hostility between Catholicism and the Revolution, thereby setting the pattern for the polarization between the Church and liberalism that continued to afflict French society. His initial assumption was that the leaders of the Revolution proposed to establish a new political and social system, and not to destroy religion. It followed that the antireligious character of 1789 was incidental and not central to the Revolution. This was true despite the fact that one of the first acts of the revolutionaries was to attack the Church, and that anticlerical passion was extinguished only slowly and with difficulty. How, then, to resolve the seeming paradox? Tocqueville did not try to minimize the extent of irreligion or its significance. He acknowledged that the philosophy of the eighteenth century was one of the principal causes of the Revolution, and that irreligion was integral to this philosophy.[16] But why, he asked, were all the men of letters antireligious, and why were they able to exert such an immense influence on the minds of others? "The spirit of Voltaire was in the world for a long time," he wrote, "but Voltaire himself could prevail only in the eighteenth century and in France."[17]

Tocqueville's explanation is that the ubiquitous hatred of Catholicism in eighteenth-century France had political, rather than religious, roots. The philosophes looked forward to complete political and social change, and because they saw the Church as a primary obstacle, they were united against it. The country at large shared this hatred of the Church as a political institution, as one of the most solid bastions of the old regime and of the entire outmoded feudal system. Hence, the attacks of the writers gained public support. But although the Church was detested because of its power and privileges, by the eighteenth century it had been weakened as a result of dependence upon the state. Religion had lent its moral authority to the secular power in exchange for material benefits. The inevitable moral followed: this state of affairs can never be advantageous to the

106

Church, which is founded on belief rather than on constraint, and it is likely to be disastrous in times of revolution.[18]

Tocqueville's entire argument, and particularly his last remark, is reminiscent of the *Démocratie*, of his conviction that the strength of religion in America derived primarily from the separation of spiritual and temporal power. He measured the religious situation in France prior to 1789 against the prototype of America, a nation that had succeeded in attaining a satisfactory relationship between religion and the modern state. It is therefore not surprising that he found the key to French antireligious sentiment in the subservience of the Church to the state, and in its willingness to surrender spiritual influence for the sake of material power. He did not, however, explicitly cite the American paradigm, offering instead other evidence to prove that it was the position of the Church that caused hostility to religion. Antireligious feeling, he noted, has declined as the Church has been forced to sever its connections with the dying institutions of the old regime. In addition, all of the Christian churches of Europe have experienced revival since the end of the revolutionary era. Tocqueville's explanation of these phenomena is at once psychological and historical. It is the common people, he asserted, who throughout history have clung to religion. Therefore democratic institutions, which are by definition responsive to the desires of the people, cannot promote irreligion. Moreover, "nothing in the Christian faith or even in Roman Catholicism is incompatible with democracy."[19] Whatever the validity of Tocqueville's interpretation of the evidence, he did not find it necessary to make any distinctions with respect to the viability of the various Christian churches in "the age of the democratic revolution." Fundamentally, his arguments reflect his conviction that religious belief is "natural" or "normal", and will resume its ascendency once the external factors causing hostility to it are removed.

At only one point did Tocqueville touch upon what might be called the "internal" factors generating antagonism towards Catholicism in pre-Revolutionary France. The philosophes realized, he wrote, that "by the very principles of its government" the Church was opposed to the ideas of eighteenth-century political theory. To the traditionalism of the Church, the Enlightenment replied with disdain for the past; the Church believed in authority over and above individual reason, while the philosophes lauded the powers of human reason; and the organization of the Church was hierarchical, thereby opposing the egalitarianism of the Enlightenment. Hence, the philosophes believed it necessary to attack the institutions

107

of the Church, which provided the foundation and model of the political and social structure they were determined to destroy. Recognition of the fact that religious and political organizations cannot be governed according to the same principles was unfortunately lacking, Tocqueville concluded.[20] He was aware of an inherent conflict between the social and political theories of the philosophes and the theories upon which the Church was based. However, he dismissed the problem rather curtly. Those characteristics of the Church that he cited—tradition, authority, and hierarchy—created, in Roger Soltau's words, "between politics and religion a conflict that was to dominate the nineteenth century."[21] To state that conflict can be avoided by recognition that the Church must be governed by these principles is beside the point, because it is precisely the effects of the differing constitutions of the Catholic Church and of the liberal state that cause the difficulty. Tocqueville tended to minimize the importance of this problem, possibly because of his conviction that the removal of Catholicism from political entanglements was a far more crucial consideration. Or is it that further probing would have forced him into an invidious comparison of Catholicism and Protestantism vis-à-vis democratization?

Tocqueville did describe the differing responses of France, England, and America to the antireligious tendencies of Enlightenment philosophy. He began by acknowledging that throughout Europe during the eighteenth century, the spiritual influence of Christianity was declining. Only in France, however, was religion actively opposed rather than simply disregarded. Moreover, outside of France irreligion was not widespread, for it was found by and large only among the upper classes. In America the antireligious features of eighteenth-century thought had little influence, despite the fact that no other country adopted the political theory of the Enlightenment to so great an extent. Tocqueville's explanation of this apparent anomaly echoes the *Démocratie:* the Americans were wise enough to realize that religion is necessary to order and stability, especially in a free society. In America antireligious doctrines were never widespread, but in England many prominent writers and thinkers became partisans of unbelief. In spite of these powerful spokesmen, the cause of irreligion did not triumph because all who feared revolution came to the defense of the established Church. Even those who were sympathetic to the religious views of the philosophes rejected them as dangerous to society. The political parties, writers, orators, and the clergy rose to defend Christianity: gradually, antireligious theories were refuted and rejected.[22]

These pages of the *Ancien Régime* were patently aimed at pointing out that the French have had to learn "in the harsh school of revolutions" that religion is necessary to society, while to the more politically sophisticated English and Americans this truth has always been evident. And yet Tocqueville was aware that the truth was far more complicated. He knew that in both England and America the nonconformist sects had helped to bring about free institutions, so that religion could not readily be considered an obstacle to political and social change. To pursue the contrast between France as opposed to England and America in these terms would, however, have meant the admission that French religious development had imposed heavy and enduring burdens. This could only be injurious to the didactic intent that played a large part in Tocqueville's discussion of religion in the *Ancien Régime,* just as it had in the *Démocratie.* In the later as well as in the earlier work he tried to teach the same lesson: hostility to the Church was caused by adventitious factors, for Catholicism was compatible with the emerging democratic societies of the West. Although it was impossible to be sanguine about the immediate prospects of French Catholicism allying itself with liberalism, the author of the *Ancien Régime* was not prepared to renounce the feasibility of this goal. Indeed, precisely because the situation in France was so unpromising, Tocqueville feared the public expression of views that might further exacerbate apathy and pessimism.[23] He was determined to believe, and he wished to persuade his countrymen to believe, that religion in its French Catholic form could work together with the "new ideas" introduced by 1789.

One of his biographers has expressed the opinion that Tocqueville was indulging in "illusions" in insisting upon the compatibility between the Catholic Church and the liberal state, at least in nineteenth-century France.[24] Certainly, Tocqueville's personal sympathy for Catholicism, together with his conviction that religion was both an individual and a social necessity, prevented him from realizing that the religious development of France was not really comparable to that of England or the United States. The crucial difference was the almost complete religious uniformity of the former, as opposed to the diversity that historical circumstances had imposed upon the English and Americans. It is curious that Tocqueville did not perceive the significance of the fact that he could quite legitimately discuss religion in France, both before and after 1789, without consideration of French Protestantism.* After the revocation of the Edict of Nantes,

*Tocqueville did at one point fleetingly refer to the Huguenot nobility of the sixteenth century, and its development of republican theories as a result of the need for religious liberty. See Tocqueville to Kergolay, Oct. 18, 1847, *Oeuvres* (B), V, p. 380.

109

Protestantism ceased to play that fertilizing and liberating role characteristic of minority religious groups. The result was intolerance and authoritarianism, not because of any ironclad determinism resulting from the
nature of Catholicism, but because lengthy and unchecked exercise of
spiritual power had produced patterns of thought and behavior incompatible with liberalism.[25] Tocqueville's belief that these patterns could be
changed with comparative rapidity, given increased independence of the
Church from the state, underestimated the depth of the emotional and
ideological cleavage that divided French society. On the other hand, his
refusal to abandon the hope that French Catholicism and liberalism might
arrive at rapprochement implied recognition that fortuitous circumstances
could modify the social and political tendencies of the various churches. He
had rejected the idea of a necessary causal relationship between religious
and political attitudes largely as a result of observation of both Catholicism
and Protestantism in England and America; and it was reasonable to
conclude that Catholicism in France was also subject to the influence of
changing conditions. Then too, his own broadly Christian loyalties and
outlook led him to look beyond the quarrels of "dévots" and anticlericals to
the fact that Christianity in all its forms shared equally those ethical and
philosophical tenets that were both valid and socially useful. And these
doctrines, whether taught by Catholicism or Protestantism, were by their
very nature compatible with that part of the Revolutionary heritage that
was also valid and socially useful. Personal beliefs thus reinforced
Tocqueville's observations and enabled him to retain the hope that the
practical obstacles impeding accommodation between French Catholicism
and "modern ideas" could be overcome.

The cutting edge of Tocqueville's interest in the relationships between
the various forms of Christianity and the social and political systems in
which they were embedded was his conviction that religion could provide
an antidote to the potentially dangerous aspects of democratization. When,
however, he turned his attention to Islam and Hinduism, it was as a
byproduct of his interest in European expansion. His advocacy of French
conquest and colonization of Algeria was, to some extent, a reflection of
domestic concerns, of his desire to stimulate French national feeling, and to
minimize the debilitating effects of individualism and materialism. But the
fundamental reason for his approval of French and British expansion in
North Africa, the Near East, and Asia, was his belief in the superiority of
Western, Christian civilization, and in its providential mission of subduing
the "stagnant" or "decadent" Eastern world.[26] It is from this perspective

that his discussions of Islam and Hinduism must be understood. Because he assumed the social and political malaise of the Muslim countries and of India, he tended to examine their religious doctrines and practices from the point of view of how they contributed to the decrepitude that justified Western domination. This mode of approach did not lead to either objective or sympathetic appraisal.

Tocqueville's judgments concerning Islam were made on the basis of his study of the Koran and of a life of Mohammed. What struck him chiefly was that this religion was much more concerned with faith, and the defense of the faith, than with setting forth specific rules of morality.[27] He stated unequivocally that the Koran was far inferior to the Gospels, since the doctrines of Mohammed were merely a compromise between gross materialism and a certain number of elevated and spiritual ideas. Violent, sensual, and egoistic tendencies predominated; and Tocqueville wondered whether the religion of the Koran could even be considered an improvement over polytheism. Compared to the latter, Islam did have a superior concept of God and of personal duties. On the other hand, polytheism allowed a freer development of human potentiality. Although he did not pursue this rather surprising comparison, his conclusion with regard to the doctrines of Mohammed was that they exercised a harmful rather than a beneficial influence. Indeed, the different destinies of the Mohammedans and Christians could be understood from a reading of the Koran and of the Gospels.[28] In the 1843 dialogue with Gobineau, Tocqueville took up this theme, since he was persuaded that his young friend displayed too much sympathy for Islam and was altogether too critical of Christianity. He assured Gobineau that, just as Christianity has helped to establish Western superiority, so Islam has been the principal cause of the decadence of the Eastern world. Thorough study of the Koran, he wrote, has convinced him that few religions are as disastrous as that of Mohammed. The social and political tendencies of Islam are far worse than those of polytheism, so that the doctrines of the Koran do not represent an improvement over ancient paganism. Perhaps wisely, Gobineau did not attempt to refute this remarkably wholesale condemnation, contenting himself with the comment that Tocqueville was "unjust" towards Islam.[29]

What is astonishing is the ease with which Tocqueville translated his studies of Muslim doctrine and practices into this dire estimate of the social and political implications of the religion of Islam. He was obviously repelled by the emphasis on faith rather than works, the duty of blind obedience, and the call to holy war, all of which he found to be part of the

111

teaching of Mohammed.[30] And yet he did not explain how these characteristics bring about deleterious political and social consequences. Only when discussing the position of the clergy in Muslim society was he able to establish a causal relationship between religious and political phenomena. He noted that among the Muslims there is no clearly defined clergy set apart from secular society, since religious and secular power were not separated. Tocqueville admitted that this absence of a priesthood was beneficial, for a sacerdotal body is the source of much "malaise social." Having extended this modicum of praise, he then returned to his usual critical stance, asserting that the union of religious and secular authority established by Mohammed was the chief cause of the despotism and social immobility endemic to Muslim societies.[31] Regardless of its validity, this judgment is concrete and meaningful: a specific religious characteristic is linked to specific social and political results. Moreover, the causal relationship that Tocqueville affirmed was one that he had tested and found valid in Western, Christian nations: the joining of religious and secular power leads to the abuse of authority and is therefore pernicious. But in this passage he was also subscribing to the time-honored dictum that the East is the natural home of despotism, maintaining that religious doctrines were primarily responsible for this situation. Montesquieu too had alleged that the religion of Islam was conducive to despotism, although he had not stressed the linkage between religious cause and political effect as explicitly as Tocqueville.[32]

Despotism in the past, "rapid and apparently unavoidable decadence" in the present and future; this was Tocqueville's depiction of Muslim societies. And while these societies have been decaying, those of the West have gained in ability and strength, so that before long all the nations of Islam will submit to Western domination.[33] It is uncertain whether Tocqueville believed that the Muslim religion itself was in decay. In his earliest essay on Algeria, written in 1837, he stated that the religious beliefs of the inhabitants were decreasing in vigor and giving way to worldly considerations.[34] This remark was made in the course of an argument designed to prove the viability of assimilation as the goal of French policy in Algeria. By 1841 he had come to believe that assimilation was not feasible, and that the proper policy was preservation of the existing society and its separation from that of the European colonists. Accordingly, he called for the maintenance and protection of Islamic schools and charitable establishments. Mohammedanism was not "absolutely impervious to

enlightenment," and the French should help it to attain the maximum possible development.[35]

Tocqueville's advocacy of the associationist theory of colonial domination carried with it significant implications. He was committed to the shoring up of a religion which, whether or not it was in a state of decay, he regarded as largely responsible for the social and political malaise of the Islamic nations. This implied acceptance of a more-or-less permanent condition of inequality, since the *moeurs* of the indigenous population of Algeria rested upon a religion that was markedly inferior to Christianity. Although he did not espouse any racial theory justifying permanent subordination of the Muslim inhabitants of Algeria, it is difficult to understand how, given his framework and assumptions, any outcome other than perpetual inequality could be envisaged.[36] In adopting the associationist theory, Tocqueville did not escape the anomalies it presented to its most well-meaning and liberal adherents. For despite its belief that indigenous institutions should be respected and preserved, associationist theory either implicitly or explicitly assumed the inferiority of these institutions. In the words of one of its later French advocates, "The policy of association . . . does not at all attempt to prepare and achieve an equality forever impossible."[37]

Tocqueville's interest in India dated from the 1840s, when he began to investigate what he considered to be the enormously important and little-known facts concerning the British conquest of India. Although a projected book on this subject never emerged beyond the stage of notes and drafts, his admiration of the rapidity and relative ease with which Britain had been able to subjugate India is apparent.[38] This feeling was matched by contempt for the passivity of the Indian response to British conquest, and he soon came to the conclusion that it was Hinduism that was responsible.[39] Confronted by a religion which, far from encouraging public spirit, led to total political indifference, Tocqueville's attitude was one of unmitigated scorn. Indeed, his criticisms of Islam appear relatively mild when compared to his almost wholly unsympathetic view of Hinduism. He was appalled, not only by the social and political consequences of the latter, but by its doctrines and moral precepts, which were more alien to him than those of Islam.

Tocqueville thought of India as a petrified society, with no change or progress in religion, philosophy, or the arts and sciences. It was also a society that had never extricated itself from the bonds of religious law and practice, so that the deleterious effects of Hinduism were enmeshed in every

113

aspect of Indian life. The caste system, an integral part of the religion itself, accounted for the lack of any sense of nationality and consequently for the ease with which invaders had always been able to conquer India. Loyalty to the nation was replaced by loyalty to one's caste, and conquerors met with resistance only when they interfered with the caste system. And, for the vast majority that belongs to the lower castes, it is immaterial who governs, since its fate has been determined by its birth. Although Tocqueville had criticized Islamic religion for its fanaticism and inclination towards holy war, he was equally censorious of Hinduism's tolerance and failure to proselytize. The latter does not persecute and convert, he argued, because it is essentially a "religion of privilege" into which one is born. As a result, it lacks any belief in human equality and in the ability of all men to know religious truth. In addition to its many harmful ideas and institutions, then, Hinduism has not even produced the kind of religious zeal that can lead a people to fight against invaders of another religion.[40]

As for the doctrines and practices of Hinduism, in Tocqueville's judgment the religion contained "the strangest mixture of some noble philosophical ideas mingled with and fused to a mass of gross absurdities."[41] He found very little that could have anything other than a pernicious effect upon morality, and he especially singled out the religion's failure to distinguish between real wrongdoing and infractions of its numerous petty practices. The doctrine of metempsychosis, together with the distinctions imposed by the caste system, accounted for the fact that the murder of a human being was not necessarily a more culpable act than the killing of a cat or dog.[42] In the midst of his condemnation of the "extravagant and degrading superstitions" that characterize Hinduism, Tocqueville frequently stated that the religion did contain remnants of highly spiritual and noble beliefs. But, instead of increasing in strength, these beliefs have decayed and been overlaid with dross. In short, Hinduism was in a state of decadence and corruption, with results so abominable that it was perhaps the only religion worth less than incredulity.[43]

Having branded Hinduism as both degenerate and socially dysfunctional, it is not surprising that Tocqueville pondered the possibility of India adopting Christianity. He was forced to admit that the prospects were not favorable, since Christianity did not appear to be making progress in India. Hinduism was able to hold its ground because it was the only link binding together the various castes. Tocqueville did not pursue this point, with its inference that Hinduism was not devoid of social utility. Instead, he asserted that India could not become civilized while Hinduism remained its religion. But how to supplant a religion that was so thoroughly intertwined with the entire complex of a society's customs and laws? The destruction of Hinduism would mean disruption of the social basis of Indian life. At best, therefore, the religion would disappear only very slowly.[44]

Given the fact that Tocqueville advocated the preservation of Islam in Algeria, his willingness to supplant Hinduism with Christianity in India poses intriguing questions. Why, for example, should conversion be desirable in India and not in Algeria? Both were, in his view, decadent societies burdened with socially dysfunctional religions. Did he see a difference between the objectives of the British in India and those of the French in Algeria? The answer to both these questions lies in the fact that Tocqueville favored an associationist policy for French Algeria, but he was convinced that Britain should pursue a policy of cultural assimilation in India. His letters to British friends in 1857, at the time of the Indian Mutiny, made the latter point obvious. In addition to endless adjurations that British defeat and withdrawal would mean delivering India to "anarchy and barbarism," he stated that the aim of Britain should be not merely to dominate India, but to civilize it.[45] He opposed the introduction of a European population into India, and this, as well as eagerness to propagate Christianity, was a hallmark of assimilationist theory. Ironically, just at the moment when the shock of the mutiny was causing Britain to reconsider the hitherto accepted policy of assimilation, Tocqueville staunchly defended it.[46] With respect to India, he could allow himself to be governed by what he evidently regarded as the humanitarian principle of rescuing India from "barbarism." The replacement of a "degraded" Hinduism by Christianity was one aspect of this civilizing mission. His approach to the French conquest and domination of Algeria, on the other hand, was that of the *homme politique*. From this point of view he decided that an associationist policy, and consequently the preservation of an admittedly inferior religion and culture, were more realistic goals.

Tocqueville's evaluations not only insist upon the socially dysfunctional effects of Islam and Hinduism, but they also imply that both religions were responsible for immutable patterns of thought and behavior. Aside from the casual remark that Islam was not utterly beyond the reach of "enlightenment," he made no allowance for the impingement of adventitious factors, for the possibility that new conditions might blunt, or even change, the effects of either of the two religions. It is this rigidity, this tendency to regard the social and political implications of both religions as fixed, that provides the sharpest contrast to his treatment of Christianity. The strength of Tocqueville's discussions of religion in Europe and America resulted from his ability to consider religious beliefs and institutions as one set of components interacting with others within a given society. Christianity neither predetermined social and political structures nor was itself derivative from material factors. Curiously, he allowed a far more strictly causative role to religion in precisely those societies that were burdened with dysfunctional religions. In the Christian West, the Churches were always at least potentially vitalizing and integrative, since they could adjust to varying social and political situations. In the non-Christian East, however, religion regularly produced despotism, social stagnation, and decay.

Tocqueville spoke of the decadence of the East, rooted as it was in religions that produced deleterious social and political institutions, as "seemingly inevitable" and "irremediable."[47] But the determinism that these words suggest was not that of any external force, such as race or climate. It was rather that the choices made by men in the past had created dysfunctional institutions, and the centuries-long grip of these institutions made change enormously difficult. Decline was far more likely, although at least theoretically not inevitable. His rejection of all theories that postulated inevitable decadence irrespective of the actions and choices of human beings is made abundantly clear in the correspondence that followed the publication of Gobineau's book on human inequality.[48] The difference between East and West was that the latter was fortunate enough to possess ideas and institutions, among them Christianity, capable of acting as barriers against decadence. But in France the burden of the past was also considerable, and, as Tocqueville's frequent warnings and strictures indicate, he was intensely aware that France might succumb to despotism, stagnation, and decline.[49] Ultimately, it was a question of the proper choices being made, and France, together with the other nations of the West, had the advantage of a religion that did not in itself produce harmful social and political consequences.

In the last analysis, Tocqueville's judgment that Islam and Hinduism were socially deleterious was the result of his definition of what constituted social dysfunction. And here, it was not simply ethnocentrism that was at work. As a moralist and a political philosopher who ranked liberty above all other social values, he was appalled by the affinity of both these Eastern religions with despotism. He had no doubt about the linkage between despotism, social stagnation, and finally decadence, and he could have no sympathy with any religion that bred this unholy trinity. In the East he saw, or thought he saw, the alliance between religion and despotism that he detested and considered a serious threat to Western societies. Hence, his criticism of Islam and Hinduism should not be regarded merely as an effort to justify Western domination. Because Tocqueville was an opponent of despotism in all its forms, he was unable to bring sympathy and detachment to his examination of the Eastern religions. His readiness to brand Islam and Hinduism as socially dysfunctional must be taken seriously, not as an appraisal of these two religions, but of the strength of his own political convictions. Similarly, his evaluations of Catholicism and Protestantism consistently turned upon the question of their ability to help the West avoid the everpresent danger of despotism that accompanied democratization. He judged that Christianity was capable of meeting this challenge, and that it could adjust to democratic conditions and promote his conception of a good society. Happily, this conclusion was acceptable to Tocqueville, the *homme politique*, for whom it was the crucial test, and to Alexis de Tocqueville, the product of a Christian society.

Notes

1. See Melvin Richter, "Comparative Political Analysis in Montesquieu and Tocqueville," *Comparative Politics*, I, no. 2 (Jan. 1969), pp. 129–160.

2. See Montesquieu, *The Spirit of the Laws*, Bk. XX, ch. 7, Bk. XXIV, ch. 5.

3. *De la démocratie en Amérique*, vol. 1, pp. 31, 34, 42; Montesquieu, *The Spirit of the Laws*, Bk. XXIV, ch. 5.

4. *De la démocratie en Amérique*, vol. 1, p. 34.

5. A recent addition to this literature provides an historical and sociological explanation of how Puritanism "produces a new kind of politics" which "sets the saints free to experiment politically." See Michael Walzer, *The Revolution of the Saints* (New York, 1970), p. 318.

6. Tocqueville, *Oeuvres* (M), Tome V, vol. 2 (*Voyages en Angleterre, Irlande, Suisse et Algérie*), pp. 24, 106, 108–110, 116, 121–123, 126, 129, 131, 143–144, 149–152, 168–169.

7. Ibid., pp. 136, 150–151.

8. Ibid., p. 51; Tocqueville to Comte Molé, May 19, 1835, *Oeuvres* (B), VI, pp. 38–39.

9. *Voyages en Angleterre, Irlande, Suisse et Algérie*, pp. 24, 27, 34, 51.

10. For this paragraph, see Ibid., p. 51; Tocqueville to Comte Molé, May 19, 1835, *Oeuvres* (B), VI, p. 39; Tocqueville to Kergolay, Oct. 18, 1847, *Oeuvres* (B), V, p. 380; *L'Ancien Régime et la Révolution*, vol. 2, pp. 334–335. See also Seymour Drescher, *Tocqueville and England* (Cambridge, Mass., 1964), ch. 3–5.

11. *Voyages en Angleterre, Irlande, Suisse et Algérie*, pp. 58–59.

12. Gertrude Himmelfarb, *Victorian Minds* (New York, 1970), p. 299.

13. Halévy, *History of the English People in the Nineteenth Century*, vol. 1, "England in 1815," pp. 389–459.

14. Tocqueville to Corcelle, July 29, 1857, *Oeuvres* (B), VI, p. 394.

15. Tocqueville to Corcelle, Aug. 5, 1857, *Oeuvres* (B), VI, pp. 394–396.

16. *L'Ancien Régime et la Révolution*, vol. 1, pp. 83, 95.

17. Ibid., p. 83.

18. Ibid., pp. 84, 203–205.

19. Ibid., p. 84.

20. Ibid., p. 204.

21. Roger Soltau, *French Political Thought in the 19th Century* (New York, 1959), p. xxviii.

22. For this paragraph, see *L'Ancien Régime et la Révolution*, vol. 1, pp. 202, 205–206.

23. Tocqueville to Gobineau, Dec. 20, 1853, Jan. 8, 1856, *Oeuvres* (M), Tome IX (op. cit.), pp. 205, 245.

24. Eichthal, op. cit., p. 52.

25. Soltau, op. cit., pp. xxvii–xxviii.

26. Tocqueville to Reeve, Apr. 12, 1840, *Oeuvres* (M), Tome VI (op. cit.), p. 58; see also Melvin Richter, "Tocqueville on Algeria," *Review of Politics*, 25, no. 3 (July 1963), pp. 385–386.

27. Tocqueville, *Oeuvres* (M), Tome III *(Ecrits et discours politiques)*, pp. 159–160.

28. Tocqueville to Kergolay, March 21, 1838, *Oeuvres* (B), V, pp. 354–356.

29. Tocqueville to Gobineau, Oct. 22, 1843, *Oeuvres* (M), Tome IX (op. cit.), pp. 68–69; Gobineau to Tocqueville, Nov. 18, 1843, *Oeuvres* (M), Tome IX (op. cit.), p. 71.

30. Tocqueville to Kergolay, March 21, 1838, *Oeuvres* (B), V, pp. 354–356; *Ecrits et discours politiques*, pp. 159–160.

31. *Ecrits et discours politiques*, p. 174.

32. Montesquieu, *The Spirit of the Laws*, Bk. XXIV, ch. 3, 4, 11, 14, also Bk. VIII, ch. 19, Bk. XII, ch. 29.

33. Tocqueville to Gobineau, Nov. 13, 1855, *Oeuvres* (M), Tome IX (op. cit.), pp. 243–244.

34. *Ecrits et discours politiques*, p. 151.

35. Tocqueville, "Rapport sur le projet de loi relatif aux crédits extraordinaires demandés pour l'Algérie," May 24, 1847, in *Ecrits et discours politiques*, pp. 323, 325.

36. On this question see Richter, op. cit., p. 365, and André Jardin, "Tocqueville et l'Algérie," *Revue des Travaux de l'Académie des sciences morales et politiques*, 4e série, 1962 (1er semestre), p. 69.

37. Jules Harmand, *Domination et colonisation* (Paris, 1910), p. 160, cited in Raymond F. Betts, *Assimilation and Association in French Colonial Theory, 1890–1914* (New York, 1961), p. 122.

38. Tocqueville to Reeve, Sept. 14, 1843, *Oeuvres* (M), Tome VI (op. cit.), p. 72; *Ecrits et discours politiques*, pp. 443–444.

39. *Ecrits et discours politiques*, pp. 449, 537.

40. For this paragraph, see Ibid., pp. 446-449, 507, 509, 542.

41. Ibid., p. 547.

42. Ibid., pp. 543-550, 552.

43. Ibid., pp. 480, 507, 543, 546.

44. For this paragraph, see Ibid., pp. 480, 502, 544, 549.

45. Tocqueville to Reeve, Aug. 2 and Sept. 22, 1857, *Oeuvres* (M), Tome VI (op. cit.), pp. 230, 236-237; Tocqueville to Senior, Aug. 6 and Nov. 15, 1857, *Correspondence and Conversations,* vol. 2, pp. 188-189, 191; Tocqueville to Lord Hatherton, Nov. 27, 1857, *Oeuvres* (B), VI, p. 423.

46. Tocqueville to Reeve, Jan. 30, 1858, *Oeuvres* (M), Tome VI (op. cit.), p. 254; see Philip D. Curtin, ed., *Imperialism* (New York, 1971), pp. xix-xx, 178-191, 285-291.

47. Tocqueville to Gobineau, Nov. 13, 1855, *Oeuvres* (M), Tome IX (op. cit.), p. 243.

48. See especially Tocqueville to Gobineau, Nov. 17, 1853, Jan. 8, 1856, *Oeuvres* (M), Tome IX (op. cit.), pp. 201-204, 244-246.

49. Koenraad W. Swart, in *The Sense of Decadence in Nineteenth-Century France* (The Hague, 1964), ch. 4, has described the increased fear of decadence in France after 1848. Tocqueville, however, rejected facile analogies between the France of Louis Napoleon and the Roman Empire. See Tocqueville to Freslon, Sept. 11, 1857, *Oeuvres* (B), VI, p. 406, and Tocqueville to Beaumont, Feb. 27, 1858, *Oeuvres* (M), Tome VIII, vol. 3, pp. 543-544.

Chapter VII

Christianity, Politics, and History:
A Summing-Up

There remain those broad and formidable questions of how Tocqueville's religious outlook shaped his work as an historian and political theorist. Was he indeed a "metahistorian," as Christopher Dawson affirms?[1] Or should his studies of Jacksonian America and of France on the eve of 1789 be described as superb historical essays of the type that Burckhardt also wrote, embodying no particular metaphysical or philosophical doctrine? And what of Halévy's comment that Tocqueville judged political questions as a "Christian moralist"?[2] Is it closer to the truth to locate his thought within the classical, secular tradition of political theory? These stark antitheses are only another way of confronting the question of the importance of religion as one motif in Tocqueville's life and thought.

The most obvious influence of his religious views on Tocqueville's historical writing might appear to be his acceptance of "Providence" as the guiding force of history. In one of the best-known passages of the *Démocratie*, he stated that during the long process of democratization in the West, "all have been blind instruments in the hands of God. The gradual development of the principle of equality is, therefore, a providential fact."[3] In the interests of precision, his definition of a "providential fact" should also be cited: "it is universal, it is lasting, it constantly eludes all human interference, and all events as well as all men contribute to its progress."[4] There are other references to the action of "Providence," or to an "unknown force" operating in the historical process, scattered throughout his writings.[5] Those who have emphasized the Christian nature of his philosophy of history have interpreted these passages to mean that he literally believed historical events to be manifestations of the will of God.[6] Other commentators, however, have insisted that his use of the term "Providence" should be understood as a metaphorical substitute for "history" or "secular development," rather than as belief in an externally planned order.[7] At least one of the older studies has concluded that Tocqueville's philosophy of history must be construed in terms of both Bossuet and Royer-Collard. He shared with the Bishop of Meaux a faith in divine intervention in human affairs, and with the Doctrinaire the conception of history as an inevitable development from the past.[8]

To suggest that Tocqueville's view of history reflected both the religious and the secular meanings of the term "Providence" is not to bury the issue in a vacuous eclecticism. In the work of many nineteenth-century historians—Guizot and Ranke come immediately to mind—it is virtually impossible to separate out "the hand of God" in history from the historicist premise of the necessary working out in the present of past tendencies and events. Nor is it faithful to the temper of mind of these historians to attempt such separation. Despite their belief that God and the historical process gave direction and meaning to the chaos of events, they nevertheless sought for the explanation of events in the actions of men. In the same way, Tocqueville's use of the term "Providence" is best understood as retaining the concept of divine guidance and sanction, while also implying a secular evolution resulting from the events of history themselves. This conclusion is scarcely surprising, since Tocqueville was greatly influenced by Guizot's historical writing, and his own apprehension of the providential element in history owed much to Guizot.[9]

To what extent, then, did Tocqueville accept one or another form of the doctrine of historical inevitability? He wrote that the general direction of history was providential and irreversible, ". . . but within these wide boundaries man is powerful and free; so too nations."[10] But precisely because his view of history was so finely balanced between the poles of freedom and necessity, the customary culling of quotations can lead to diverse conclusions. It is, therefore, more profitable to recall how he defined the possibilities and limitations of human action in the course of discussing a specific historical phenomenon, for example, that of decadence. Although evidently convinced that, for all practical purposes, decadence was unavoidable in Hindu and Muslim societies, he did not argue that either metaphysical or material forces had predestined certain areas of the world to stagnation and decay. It was rather that the long-range effects of deeply imbedded ideas and institutions had proven to be socially deleterious and therefore must lead to decay, unless change could be achieved. Given sufficient human wisdom, decadence was at least potentially reversible, just as human choice and action had originally produced and preserved dysfunctional ideas and institutions. What emerges, then, is that the historical process creates its own long-range trends, but that man had the capacity to influence, and even to control, these general tendencies. When? How? To what extent? These questions could be answered only within the context of a particular historical situation. For example, tendencies towards decadence in France could be reversed more readily than those in India or Algeria, since there were many more factors in the French past and present militating against decadence. This is neither the "Cleopatra's nose" theory of history nor a rigid historical determinism. It corresponds to the working historian's sense of the interplay between human action and larger causal trends within the historical process. If Tocqueville's view of history is understood in this way, it becomes evident how he could insist upon free will, condemn all forms of historical determinism, and yet indulge in predictions on such subjects as decadence and democratization. His predictions were not based on presumably fixed laws from which "necessary" or "inevitable" events could be deduced, but upon his estimate of the strength and viability of existent trends and conditions within a given society.[11]

To characterize Tocqueville as a "metahistorian" who saw historical events as explicit and preordained manifestations of the will of God is excessive, although there are vestiges of this Christian philosophy of history in his thought. Religious influences reveal themselves more subtly and yet more pervasively in what Pierson has described as his "belief in the superior desirability and effectiveness of moral forces."[12] It was the human capacity for noble and selfless actions that he esteemed, and he judged the protagonists in the historical drama in terms of these standards. Although this kind of moral earnestness need not be linked to religion, Tocqueville associated it with Christian ethics and philosophy. The consequence was not only rejection of historical determinism and emphasis on the ability of men to choose between good and evil, but a tendency to evaluate historical actions in terms of their spiritual and moral content. The shortcomings of this approach betrayed themselves in the inadequate attention that Tocqueville paid to economic factors in both the *Démocratie* and the *Ancien Régime*.[13] He regarded economic life as par excellence "material," and intrinsically less worthy of serious attention than politics. The latter did, after all, deal with the moral problems and choices of men in society.

In truth, Tocqueville held that "heroic view of history," as Lively calls it, which, according to the *Démocratie*, characterized aristocratic epochs.[14] But this "heroic view" was essentially a moral view, derived ultimately from his personal religious outlook. The actions of men had historical significance, and these actions were affected by ideas, passions, and beliefs, as well as by the brute facts of material reality. The influence of ideas in history, with the inference that human beings did exercise choice, was repeatedly stressed by Tocqueville.[15] Since there were no fixed laws that determined the role of ideas in history, only careful study of a limited topic could reveal the interplay of ideas and social structure in a given society. And in the *Démocratie*, in the *Souvenirs*, and in the *Ancien Régime*, Tocqueville did examine the nature of this interaction with notable delicacy and balance. Although his religiously based idealism prevented him from coping with the role of economic factors, it did have beneficial results. It led him to seriously consider the claims of human beings, their ideas and choices, within the historical process.

The relationship between Tocqueville's religious outlook and his views as a political theorist, complex enough in itself, has at times become grist for various ideological mills. Many of the older studies, which presented him as a nineteenth-century political liberal, tended to ignore or denigrate the importance of religion in his life and work.[16] Other commentary has taken the position that Tocqueville was indeed a Christian moralist, and that his religious and philosophical premises identify him as a "liberal-conservative," if not as an outright conservative.[17] A new fillip was added to the pleasures of controversy with the appearance of two analytical studies that suggested that religion played a significant role in Tocqueville's thought, but for purely pragmatic rather than personal reasons.[18] The crux of this interpretation is that he regarded religion as a socially useful myth, to be inculcated as a means of insuring stability amid the flux of democratic societies. Although this argument does have the merit of taking Tocqueville's functional approach seriously, it does not follow that because he was concerned with the social effects of religious beliefs, he considered religion "solely from the point of view of these effects," or that he advocated "the propagation of spiritualistic myths."[19]

Perhaps the chief lesson to be derived from close examination of Tocqueville's religious outlook is the inextricable meshing in his mind of "faith," "truth," and "utility." His tendency to consider religion "from a

124

human point of view" cannot be divorced from personal factors, from the desire to find a means of confirming the human need for faith and therefore the "truth" of religion. This, too, may be myth-making, but it is very different from the deliberate deception of asking others to accept a social myth that is admittedly false. In any case, this was a mode of thought common to many in early nineteenth-century France. Their objective was not to impose a social myth, but to ground religious belief upon psychological verities, since they could not accept the certitudes of Catholic theology.

Does it then follow that Tocqueville believed all religions to be beneficial "from a human point of view," regardless of their inherent worth or validity?[20] In the *Démocratie* he did state more-or-less explicitly that any religion was better than none, and yet his appraisals of Islam and Hinduism were not consistent with this conclusion.[21] He declared both religions to be socially pernicious, and branded Hinduism a religion worth less than unbelief. Overtly, his criteria were those of social utility, but it was in terms of Christian standards that he judged the Eastern religions to be spiritually and morally deficient, and therefore socially deleterious. In short, his functionalism was more apparent than real, since he was unable to separate out his own belief in the superiority of Christian values when he was confronted by alien norms and practices.

No such discrepancy between his private convictions and an austere functionalism muddied his analysis when Tocqueville dealt with any religion within the vague confines of Christianity. He took it for granted that all of the various Christian creeds embodied certain basic religious truths, answered to human needs, and were at least potentially socially useful. Hence, it was possible for him to compare the actual performances of American Protestantism and Catholicism, the Anglican Church and the sects, and French and Irish Catholicism, from the point of view of social function. These were not social myths to be preserved, but genuine religions teaching the existence of God, the immortality of the soul, and the ethics of the Gospel. Because they did teach these truths, albeit amid much dross, they were also beneficial to the individual and to society. To this extent, then, the appellation of "Christian moralist" is warranted, since for Tocqueville it was Christian ethical and philosophical precepts, defined in a broad nondoctrinal sense, that provided the touchstone of both truth and utility.

The effects of this point of view upon his political theory do not lend themselves to any simple ideological classification. Tocqueville the

"Christian moralist" and Tocqueville the social theorist were agreed that religion was a necessary means of social integration, especially in modern, democratic societies. It can be argued that this stress on the integrative function of religion is prima facie evidence of political conservatism. But this is to ignore Robert Merton's cogent remark that "integration is a plainly formal concept. A society may be integrated around norms of strict caste, regimentation, and docility of subordinated social strata, just as it may be integrated around norms of open mobility, wide areas of self-expression and independence of judgment."[22] The belief that religion is a desirable means of assuring social integration does not constitute proof of conservatism, or indeed of any specific ideological stance, until substantive questions are answered. What is the nature of the society that is to be integrated by religion? Is religion to integrate a society by means of manipulation and coercion, or through belief and persuasion? Is the religion so authoritarian that it can sustain only an authoritarian society? There is no doubt that Tocqueville favored a society in which liberty, political participation, and legal guarantees against arbitrary power would exist; a society that in some broad sense of the word must be defined as "liberal." In such a society the claims of religion had to be freely accepted by the individual, and established through belief rather than manipulation or coercion.[23] As for religion by definition promoting authoritarianism, Tocqueville was convinced that all forms of Christianity were compatible with a liberal society. In itself, then, his belief that religion ought to integrate a society around a system of fixed norms and values is not an indication of a flawed liberalism.

Nor is Tocqueville's attitude towards religion and social conflict amenable to the interpretation that he saw religion as a means of preventing social and political change. His treatment of church–state relations in the United States and in pre-Revolutionary France is a gloss upon the text that religion must remain neutral amid the quarrels and turmoil of political life. Not only was he unwilling to allow to secular institutions the sanctification and support of religion; he knew well that the absolute values of religion itself could act as a solvent of social and political stability. Indeed, during the Second Empire he came close to condoning disobedience to the established regime in the name of a religiously based code of public morality. His knowledge of the seventeenth-century English revolutions, as well as of the American colonial experience, taught Tocqueville to separate the stabilizing moral and psychological influence of religious belief from its possibly disruptive effects upon established institutions. As a result, he did not share the feelings of those who, whether in a spirit of satisfaction or of hostility, considered religion the preordained enemy of social and political change.

Perhaps use of the term "moral integration," rather than "social integration," helps to avert misconceptions and comes closer to expressing Tocqueville's views. Instability and even revolution seemed to him characteristic of the process of democratization in the West. If change could be restricted to the social and political arena, the democratic revolution would be less than "total," and its consequences less burdensome.[24] The cost of total revolution was high: loss of norms and restraints, leading to wholesale innovation and destruction. Because they retained religious belief, the English and Americans avoided this kind of cataclysm. But in France religion unfortunately lost its hold before 1789. Subsequently, the nation underwent a total revolution, with protracted and damaging repercussions. The lesson was evident. By acting as a source of moral cohesiveness, rather than by pronouncing upon the merits of specific social and political institutions, the various Christian churches could ameliorate the effects of the democratic revolution. The question of the relationship between this point of view and Tocqueville's ideological affinities is ultimately one of definition. Nevertheless, understanding of what he himself meant in stressing the integrative role of religion in society does appear to preclude any facile identification with political conservatism.[25]

In his recent study of the history of Western political thought, Sheldon Wolin referred to that "sociological appreciation of religion," which appeared at the beginning of the nineteenth century and which has extended into the twentieth century.[26] And this "appreciation" is linked to the desire to recapture a sense of community in an atomized and ceaselessly changing society. Wolin has also shown how these themes are to be found in theorists of the most diverse ideological persuasions.[27] It is within this frame of reference that the place of religion in Tocqueville's political and social thought can best be understood. He too saw "the sacred," envisaged as an innate part of human consciousness, as a means of coping with problems that were fundamentally moral and psychological, rather than political. Perhaps it was his own personal life experience—his anomalous position with respect to Catholicism and his awareness of belonging to a moribund social class—that sensitized him to those modern maladies of anomie and rootlessness. In any event, he cast his net wider than the familiar terrors of institutional instability and political revolution, emphasizing the ability of religion to counter the effects of social change and personal demoralization.

Wolin described the tendency to assert the importance of religion, community, and society, prevalent from Maistre to Durkheim, as "the sublimation of politics."[28] This phrase is not applicable to Tocqueville's thought. Although he did stake out large claims for the benefits that religion could render to modern societies, he was equally vehement in proclaiming that political life held out efficacious means of combating the dangers of democratization. He did not regard the two sets of claims as incompatible. All of the political and institutional devices that he recommended—the jury system, a free press, decentralization, increased political participation—were really means of creating a politically active and involved citizenry. He shared the Greek view that political life was inherently dignifying, and that participation in it elevates men from the material preoccupations of daily life. Democracies, which were particularly prone to the corrosive effects of egoistic individualism and of materialism, must do everything possible to encourage what has been termed "the life of citizenship."[29] But to be a good citizen, to participate in politics, means to believe that there exists a shared set of norms that act as rules of the game, legitimatizing political action. Tocqueville was convinced that these norms could only be provided by religion. In order to operate properly, the political and institutional mechanisms that he advocated had to be supported by a religious scaffolding. Conversely, without the proper institutional framework and a rich civic life, the moral authority of religion could, by itself, accomplish nothing. It might, in fact, be detrimental, as the example of the Second Empire proved. In Tocqueville's social and political theory both religion and political participation are held in balance as the two irreducible elements necessary to a good society.

To reach this conclusion is to take Tocqueville at his own word: he repeatedly asserted the importance of both religion and free institutions. He was not alone in professing this dual loyalty, but there were few for whom the enterprise of yoking together liberty and religion appeared at once so crucial and yet so precarious. What remained at issue was whether, in fact as well as in theory, the Christian churches of the West would be able to act as a source of moral stability. Could genuine religious faith—for nothing less would do—continue to exist amid the unceasing intellectual and material flux that accompanied democratization? Ultimately this was a matter of individual choice, and the outcome of this "trial of faith" could not be predicted.[30] Much depended upon the behavior of the churches themselves, upon their ability to gain a position above and beyond the strife of parties, classes, and governments. The churches in England and

America provided evidence that Christianity could successfully pass this different kind of trial, but in France this was unhappily not yet the case. Hence, Tocqueville's efforts, both in his public life and in his writings, to persuade French Catholicism to rid itself of political entanglements and of fear of modernity. By the end of his life he was disabused of any hope that the accommodation of Catholicism to post-Revolutionary French society would come about either rapidly or easily.

Could his endeavors have been more successful, if not immediately, then in terms of establishing a tradition that proclaimed the possibility of reconciliation between French Catholicism and liberalism? For in this respect, as in so many others, Tocqueville had no intellectual heirs.[31] Even Vacherot and Prévost-Paradol, who were in many respects influenced by his ideas, did not agree that organized religion was the indispensable means of assuring moral stability to France. Other liberals, for example Jules Simon and Renouvier, also abandoned any thought of conciliation with the Church. Instead, they pronounced in favor of a secular, although not atheistic, morality which could inculcate the necessary norms and values.[32] In the years after Tocqueville's death, only a small band of liberal Catholics continued to espouse views similar to his, and their voices carried no weight among those who were fashioning the anticlerical ideology of the Third Republic.

The irony is that Tocqueville's consciousness of the precarious position of liberty and religion, not only in France but potentially throughout the West, imposed reticences and hesitations that weakened his efforts. He could not allow himself the temerity of a Lord Acton, secure in his Catholic faith and in the moral and political cohesion of English society. The latter had no hesitation in freely anathematizing all enemies of liberty, not least those within his own Church. Tocqueville was neither emotionally nor intellectually prepared to risk devastating onslaughts which might provide ready ammunition to the enemies of either liberty or religion. But without boldness and incesiveness—the qualities that were lacking in his efforts as a publicist and in his political career—his call for rapprochement between French Catholicism and a liberal society could awaken no enthusiasm and found no echoes.

The historian and political theorist, however, can only welcome his sensitive and probing analysis of the "trial" that confronted the various Christian churches, and indeed religious faith itself, in the democratic societies of the West. Just as mention of Lord Acton underlines Tocqueville's weaknesses and timidities, so too does the same comparison point

129

up the strengths of the latter. For Lord Acton's certainties seem to belong to another world, an irreclaimable world of moral and political stability. Tocqueville knew this world was lost, and feared that liberty and religion might well also be lost. In this respect, he was far more modern than Lord Acton, far more aware of the difficulties posed by democratization. And so he undertook a kind of exploratory mission among the religions of the West, to determine their viability in the new democratic world and their ability to work in harmony with free institutions. His aim was to understand in order to act, but in the last years of his life he seemed finally to be aware that the task of understanding was his true métier.

Notes

1. Christopher Dawson, *Dynamics of World History* (New York, 1956), p. 292. Hayden White's recent discussion of Tocqueville in his *Metahistory. The Historical Imagination in Nineteenth-Century Europe* (Baltimore, 1973), ch. 5, is not concerned with the religious implications of Tocqueville's historical work.

2. Elie Halévy, *History of the English People in the Nineteenth Century,* vol. 4, "Victorian Years," p. 406.

3. *De la démocratie en Amérique,* vol. 1, p. 4.

4. Ibid.

5. Tocqueville, "Discours de réception à l'Académie française," April 21, 1842, *Oeuvres* (B), IX, p. 22; *L'Ancien Régime et la Révolution,* vol. 1, pp. 73–74; Tocqueville to Gobineau, Nov. 13, 1855, *Oeuvres* (M), Tome IX (op. cit.), pp. 243–244.

6. Dawson, op. cit., pp. 292–293; Redier, op. cit., pp. 222–224; Albert Salomon, "Tocqueville's Philosophy of Freedom," *Review of Politics,* I (1939), p. 410.

7. Drescher, *Dilemmas,* pp. 27–28, 268, 278; Georges Lefebvre, "Introduction," *L'Ancien Régime et la Révolution,* vol. 1, pp. 23–24; Jack Lively, *The Social and Political Thought of Alexis de Tocqueville* (Oxford, 1962), pp. 33–34. Drescher (p. 28) does however state that Tocqueville's use of the term "providential" implies "sanction by divine plan." Marvin Zetterbaum, in *Tocqueville and the Problem of Democracy* (Stanford, 1967), offers an interpretation that fits into neither of these categories, since he argues that Tocqueville used the idea of Providence or, as Zetterbaum calls it, "the inevitability thesis," as a "salutary myth" (pp. 19, 147). The purpose of this strategy, according to Zetterbaum, was that "By assigning the defense of democracy to history or Providence, he removed himself from the partisan fray," and yet was able to promote the democratic cause (p. 20). Since Tocqueville used the word "Providence" in other contexts beside that of democratization, I do not see that the Zetterbaum interpretation, irrespective of its other difficulties, solves the problem of what Tocqueville meant by "Providence."

8. Marcel, op. cit., pp. 83, 87.

9. Edward T. Gargan, "Tocqueville and the Problem of Historical

Prognosis," *American Historical Review*, LXVIII, no. 2 (Jan. 1963), p. 335; also Gargan, *De Tocqueville* (London, 1965), pp. 26-32.

10. *De la démocratie en Amérique,* vol. 2, p. 339.

11. This is essentially the same conclusion as that reached by Gargan, in "Tocqueville and the Problem of Historical Prognosis," op. cit., pp. 332-345, and Lively, op. cit., pp. 32-40.

12. Pierson, *Tocqueville and Beaumont in America,* p. 762.

13. This weakness has been noticed by many commentators. See Drescher, *Dilemmas,* pp. 65-71; Lively, op. cit., p. 251; Pierson, op. cit., pp. 762-763.

14. Lively, op. cit., p. 38.

15. *L'Ancien Régime et la Révolution,* vol. 1, pp. 83, 193-201; Tocqueville to Bouchitté, Sept. 23, 1853, Tocqueville to Odilon Barrot, July 18, 1856, *Oeuvres* (B), VII, pp. 299, 395; Tocqueville to Corcelle, Oct. 16, 1855, *Oeuvres* (B), VI, p. 301; Tocqueville, "Discours de réception à l'Académie française," April 21, 1842, "Discours prononcé à la séance publique annuelle de l'Académie des sciences morales et politiques," April 5, 1852, *Oeuvres* (B), IX, pp. 5-6, 123.

16. Eichthal, op. cit.; Marcel, op. cit.; Guido de Ruggiero, *The History of European Liberalism* (Boston, 1959), pp. 187-197; Soltau, op. cit., pp. 50-56.

17. J. P. Mayer, *Alexis de Tocqueville* (New York, 1940), esp. pp. 163-169; Redier, op. cit.; Salomon, op. cit., esp. pp. 402, 413; Salomon, "Tocqueville, Moralist and Sociologist," *Social Research,* II (1935), pp. 405-427.

18. Lively, op. cit., pp. 183-203; Zetterbaum, op. cit., pp. 109-123.

19. Lively, op. cit., p. 197; Zetterbaum, op. cit., p. 122.

20. This is the interpretation suggested by Zetterbaum, op. cit., pp. 121-122, notes.

21. *De la démocratie en Amérique,* vol. 2, pp. 151-152.

22. Robert K. Merton, *Social Theory and Social Structure* (Glencoe, 1957), p. 44.

23. Lively, op. cit., p. 197, arguing from the position that Tocqueville saw religion as social myth, states that there is an inconsistency between Tocqueville's "basic plea for liberty" and his views on religion.

24. This aspect of Tocqueville's thought has been studied by Melvin Richter, "Tocqueville's Contribution to the Theory of Revolution," in Carl Friedrich, ed., *Revolution* (New York, 1966), pp. 75-121.

25. In the course of an original and highly sophisticated analysis of Tocqueville's historical writing, White (op. cit., p. 193) concludes that Tocqueville's "specific style of historical reflection . . . is not exhaustively describable in terms of a given ideological label (such as Liberal or Conservative)."

26. Sheldon S. Wolin, *Politics and Vision* (Boston, 1960), pp. 366-368.

27. Ibid., pp. 357-376.

28. Ibid., p. 353.

29. Melvin Richter, *The Politics of Conscience. T. H. Green and his Age* (London, 1964), p. 345.

30. Drescher, in *Dilemmas,* p. 29, note, suggests the same point when he remarks that Tocqueville regarded religion as "problematic."

31. Raymond Aron, in "Les grandes Doctrines de sociologie historique," *Cours de Sorbonne* (Paris, n.d.), p. 176, remarks upon this point.

32. There is as yet no satisfactory treatment of this important subject.

Relevant information may be found in the following: Henri Michel, *L'Idée de l'Etat* (Paris, 1898); John A. Scott, *Republican Ideas and the Liberal Tradition in France, 1870-1914* (New York, 1951); Soltau, op. cit., pp. 251-261, 295-321; Etienne Vacherot, *La Démocratie* (Paris, 1860), pp. 41-65; Weill, *Histoire de l'idée laïque en France au XIXe siècle.*

Bibliography

This is not a complete listing of the various editions of Tocqueville's works, or of the secondary literature about Tocqueville. Only those books and articles used in the preparation of this study are cited. For fuller bibliographies see the following, all of which are cited below: the Bradley and the Mayer and Lerner editions of *Democracy in America;* Drescher, *Tocqueville and England;* Pierson, *Tocqueville and Beaumont in America.*

I. Manuscript Sources

Procès-verbaux du Comité de Constitution de 1848, 19 mai–17 juin 1848. Archives nationales, C9I8.

Yale Tocqueville Collection. Beinecke Library, Yale University. Pierson, in *Tocqueville and Beaumont in America,* provides a description of this Collection. The Collection itself now includes an updated and detailed catalogue.

II. Newspapers and Government Documents

Le Commerce, July 1844–May 1845.

Compte rendu des séances de l'Assemblée nationale, 11 vols. Paris, 1849–1850.

Le Moniteur universel, 1839–1851.

Le Siècle, July 1844–May 1845.

III. The Works of Alexis de Tocqueville

Correspondence and Conversations of Alexis de Tocqueville with Nassau William Senior from 1834 to 1859, ed. by M. C. M. Simpson. 2 vols. London, 1872.

Democracy in America. Translation by Henry Reeve. Revised by Francis Bowen. Edited by Phillips Bradley. 2 vols. New York, 1945 (paperback edition, 2 vols., New York, 1954).

Democracy in America. Translated by George Lawrence. Edited by J.-P. Mayer and Max Lerner. 1 vol. New York, 1966.

Oeuvres complètes. Edited by Gustave de Beaumont. 9 vols. Paris, 1860–1866.

Vol. I-III.	*De la démocratie en Amérique.*
Vol. IV.	*L'Ancien Régime et la Révolution.*
Vol. V-VI.	*Oeuvres et correspondance inédites.*
Vol. VII.	*Nouvelle correspondance entièrement inédite.*
Vol. VIII.	*Mélanges, fragments historiques et notes sur l'Ancien Régime, la Révolution et l'Empire, voyages, pensées entièrement inédits.*
Vol. IX.	*Etudes économiques politiques et littéraires.*

Oeuvres complètes, édition définitive publiée sous la direction de J.-P. Mayer. Paris, 1951–.

Tome I.	*De la démocratie en Amérique.* 2 vols. (1951). Introduction par Harold J. Laski.
Tome II.	*L'Ancien Régime et la Révolution.* 2 vols. (1953). Introduction par Georges Lefebvre. Vol. 2 is subtitled *Fragments et notes inédites sur la Révolution.* Texte établi et annoté par André Jardin.
Tome III.	*Ecrits et discours politiques.* Vol. 1 (1962). Introduction par J.-J. Chevallier et André Jardin. Texte établi et annoté par André Jardin.
Tome V.	Vol. 1. *Voyages en Sicile et aux Etats-Unis.* (1957). Texte établi, annoté et préfacé par J.-P. Mayer. Vol. 2. *Voyages en Angleterre, Irlande, Suisse et Algérie.* (1958). Texte établi et annoté par J.-P. Mayer et André Jardin.
Tome VI.	*Correspondance anglaise.* Vol. 1 (1954). *Correspondance d'Alexis de Tocqueville avec Henry Reeve et John Stuart Mill.* Introduction par J.-P. Mayer. Texte établi et annoté par J.-P Mayer et Gustave Rudler.
Tome VIII.	*Correspondance d'Alexis de Tocqueville et de Gustave de Beaumont.* 3 vols. (1967). Texte établi, annoté et préfacé par André Jardin.
Tome IX.	*Correspondance d'Alexis de Tocqueville et d'Arthur de Gobineau.* (1959). Introduction par J.-J. Chevallier. Texte établi et annoté par M. Degros.
Tome XI.	*Correspondance d'Alexis de Tocqueville avec P.-P. Royer-Collard et avec J.-J. Ampère.* (1970). Texte établi, annoté et préfacé par André Jardin.
Tome XII.	*Souvenirs.* (1964). Texte établi, annoté et préfacé par Luc Monnier.

"Profession de foi," March 19, 1848, in *Assemblée constituante, élections, la Manche, 1848.*

Quelques correspondants de Mr. et Mrs. Childe. London, 1912.

The Recollections of Alexis de Tocqueville. Translated by Alexander Teixeira de Mattos. Edited by J. P. Mayer. New York, 1959.

IV. Other Books and Articles

Acomb, Evelyn M. and Brown, Marvin L., eds. *French Society and Culture Since the Old Regime.* New York, 1966.

Ahlstrom, Sydney E. *A Religious History of the American People.* New Haven, 1972.

Alexis de Tocqueville: Livre du centenaire, 1859-1959. Paris, 1960.

Alméras, Charles. *Odilon Barrot.* Paris, 1950.

Arendt, Hannah. *The Human Condition.* Chicago, 1958.

Aron, Raymond. "Les grandes Doctrines de sociologie historique." *Cours de Sorbonne.* Paris, n.d.

——. "Idées politiques et vision historique de Tocqueville," *Revue française de sciences politiques,* X (Sept. 1960), pp. 509-526.

Aubert, Roger. *Le Pontificat de Pie IX.* Paris, 1952.

Bailyn, Bernard. *The Ideological Origins of the American Revolution.* Cambridge, Mass., 1967.

Barrot, Odilon. *Mémoires posthumes.* 4 vols. Paris, 1875-1876.

Bastid, Paul. *Doctrines et institutions politiques de la seconde république.* 2 vols. Paris, 1945.

Baunard, Louis. *La foi et ses victoires dans le siècle présent.* 2 vols. Paris, 1884.

Beaumont, Gustave de. *Lettres d'Amérique, 1831-1832.* Edited by A. Jardin and G. W. Pierson. Paris, 1973.

——. *Marie, ou l'esclavage aux Etats-Unis.* Paris, 1835.

——, and Tocqueville, Alexis de. *Du système pénitentiaire aux Etats-Unis.* Paris, 1833.

Bellah, Robert N. "Civil Religion in America." *Daedalus* (Winter 1967), pp. 1-21.

Bertier de Sauvigny, G. de. *La Restauration.* Paris, 1955.

Betts, Raymond F. *Assimilation and Association in French Colonial Theory, 1890-1914.* New York, 1961.

Biddiss, Michael D. "Prophecy and Pragmatism: Gobineau's Confrontation with Tocqueville." *The Historical Journal,* XIII, no. 4 (1970), pp. 611-633.

Boas, George. *French Philosophies of the Romantic Period.* New York, 1964.

Boorstin, Daniel J. *The Genius of American Politics.* Chicago, 1958.

Bourgeois, Emile, and Clermont, Emile. *Rome et Napoléon III.* Paris, 1907.

Brogan, D. W. *Citizenship Today.* Chapel Hill, 1960.

Brogan, Hugh. *Tocqueville.* London, 1973.

Callier, Camille. *Lettres du Col. Callier.* Edited by A. B. Duff and M. Degros. Paris, 1950.

du Camp, Maxime. *Souvenirs de l'année 1848.* Paris, 1876.

Charléty, S. C. G. *La Monarchie de Juillet, 1830-1848.* Paris, 1921.

Charlton, D. G. *Secular Religions in France, 1815–1870.* London, 1963.

Craven, Wesley Frank. *The Legend of the Founding Fathers.* New York, 1956.

Curtin, Philip D., ed. *Imperialism.* New York, 1971.

Dansette, Adrien. *Histoire religieuse de la France contemporaine.* Paris, 1965.

———. *Louis Napoléon à la conquête du pouvoir.* Paris, 1961.

Daumard, Adeline. *La bourgeoisie parisienne de 1815 à 1848.* Paris, 1963.

Davis, David Brion. *The Problem of Slavery in Western Culture.* Cornell, 1969.

Dawson, Christopher. *Dynamics of World History.* New York, 1956.

Diez del Corral, Luis. *La Mentalidad Politica de Tocqueville con especial referencia a Pascal.* Madrid, 1965.

Drescher, Seymour. *Dilemmas of Democracy. Tocqueville and Modernization.* Pittsburgh, 1968.

———, ed. *Tocqueville and Beaumont on Social Reform.* New York, 1968.

———. *Tocqueville and England.* Cambridge, Mass., 1964.

Dreyfus, Ferdinand. *L'Assistance sous la seconde république.* Paris, 1907.

Duroselle, J.-B. *Les Débuts du catholicisme social en France (1822–1870).* Paris, 1951.

d'Eichthal, Eugène. *Alexis de Tocqueville et la Démocratie libérale.* Paris, 1897.

Evans, David Owen. *Social Romanticism in France, 1830–1848.* Oxford, 1951.

Falloux, Alfred de. *Mémoires d'un royaliste.* 3 vols. Paris, 1925.

———. *Mme. Swetchine, sa vie et ses oeuvres.* 2 vols. Paris, 1860.

Friedrich, Carl. *Revolution.* New York, 1966.

Gargan, Edward T. *Alexis de Tocqueville: The Critical Years, 1848–1851.* Washington, D.C., 1955.

———. *De Tocqueville.* London, 1965.

———. "Tocqueville and the Problem of Historical Prognosis." *American Historical Review,* LXIII, no. 2 (Jan. 1963), pp. 332–345.

Gay, Peter. *The Party of Humanity.* New York, 1964.

Gerbod, Paul. *La condition universitaire en France aux XIX ͤ siècle.* Paris, 1965.

Girard, Louis. *La II ͤ République.* Paris, 1968.

Goldstein, Doris S. "Alexis de Tocqueville's Concept of Citizenship." *Proceedings of the American Philosophical Society,* vol. 180, no. 1 (Feb. 1964), pp. 39–53.

———. " 'Official Philosophies' in Modern France: The Example of Victor Cousin." *Journal of Social History,* I (Spring 1968), pp. 259–279.

———. "The Religious Beliefs of Alexis de Tocqueville." *French Historical Studies,* I, no. 4 (Fall 1960), pp. 379–393.

de la Gorce, Pierre. *Histoire de la seconde République française.* 2 vols. Paris, 1919.

Grimaud, Louis. *Histoire de la liberté d'enseignement en France.* Tome 6, *La Monarchie de Juillet.* Paris, 1954.

Hales, E. E. Y. *Pio Nono.* New York, 1954.

Halévy, Elie. *History of the English People in the Nineteenth Century.* 6 vols. London, 1951.

Hartman, Mary S. "The Sacrilege Law of 1825 in France: A Study in Anticlericalism and Mythmaking." *Journal of Modern History*, 44, no. 1 (March 1972), pp. 21–37.

Hartz, Louis. *The Liberal Tradition in America.* New York, 1955.

Herr, Richard. *Tocqueville and the Old Regime.* Princeton, 1962.

Higham, John. "The Cult of the 'American Consensus': Homogenizing Our History." *Commentary*, XXVII (Feb. 1959), pp. 93–100.

Higonnet, Patrick L.-R., and Higonnet, Trevor B. "Class, Corruption, and Politics in the French Chamber of Deputies, 1846–1848." *French Historical Studies*, V, no. 2 (Fall 1967), pp. 204–224.

Himmelfarb, Gertrude. *Lord Acton. A Study in Conscience and Politics.* London, 1952.

——. *Victorian Minds.* New York, 1970.

Huckaby, John K. "Roman Catholic Reaction to the Falloux Law." *French Historical Studies*, IV (Fall 1965), pp. 203–213.

Hudson, Winthrop S. *American Protestantism.* Chicago, 1961.

Jardin, André, and Tudesq André-Jean. *La France des notables.* 2 vols. Paris, 1973.

Jardin, André. "Tocqueville et l'Algérie." *Revue des Travaux de l'Académie des sciences morales et politiques*, 4e série, 1962 (1er semestre), pp. 61–74.

Johnson, Douglas. *Guizot.* London and Toronto, 1963.

Lebey, André. *Louis Napoléon Bonaparte et le ministère Odilon Barrot.* Paris, 1912.

Lecanuet, Edouard. *Montalembert.* 3 vols. Paris, 1895–1902.

Lipset, Seymour M. *The First New Nation.* New York, 1963.

——. *Political Man.* New York, 1960.

Lively, Jack. *The Social and Political Thought of Alexis de Tocqueville.* London, 1962.

Lukacs, John. "The Last Days of Alexis de Tocqueville." *Catholic Historical Review*, L, no. 2 (July 1964), pp. 155–170.

de Luna, Frederick A. *The French Republic under Cavaignac, 1848.* Princeton, 1969.

Marcel, R.-P. *Essai politique sur Alexis de Tocqueville.* Paris, 1910.

Marcilhacy, Christianne. *Le diocèse d'Orléans au milieu du XIXe siècle.* Paris, 1964.

Marshall, Lynn L., and Drescher, Seymour. "American Historians and Tocqueville's *Democracy.*" *Journal of American History*, LV, no. 3 (Dec. 1968), pp. 512–532.

Marshall, T. H. *Class, Citizenship and Social Development.* New York, 1964.

May, Anita Rasi. "The Falloux Law, the Catholic Press, and the Bishops: Crisis of Authority in the French Church." *French Historical Studies*, VIII (Spring 1973), pp. 77–94.

Mayer, J. P. *Alexis de Tocqueville.* New York, 1940.

Mayeur, J. M. "Catholicisme intransigeant, Catholicisme social, démocratie chrétienne." *Annales*, Mars-Avril 1972, pp. 483–499.

Mead, Sidney. *The Lively Experiment.* New York, 1963.

Merton, Robert K. *Social Theory and Social Structure.* Glencoe, 1957.

Michel, Henri. *L'Idée de l'Etat.* Paris, 1898.

——. *La loi Falloux.* Paris, 1906.

Montesquieu, Charles de. *Considerations on the Greatness and Decline of the Romans.*

Translated by David Lowenthal. New York, 1965.

___. *The Spirit of the Laws.* Translated by Thomas Nugent. Introduction by Franz Neumann. New York, 1966.

Moody, Joseph N. "The French Catholic Press in the Education Conflict of the 1840's." *French Historical Studies,* VII, no. 2 (Spring 1972), pp. 394–414.

Nisbet, Robert. *The Quest for Community.* New York, 1953.

___. *The Sociological Tradition.* New York, 1967.

Pierson, George Wilson. *The Moving American.* New York, 1973.

___. *Tocqueville and Beaumont in America.* New York, 1938. Abridged by Dudley C. Lunt as *Tocqueville in America,* with a new Bibliographical Note. Garden City, 1959.

Poggi, Gianfranco. *Images of Society. Essays on the Sociological Theories of Tocqueville, Marx, and Durkheim.* Stanford, 1972.

Pouthas, Charles. *Guizot pendant la Restauration.* Paris, 1923.

Redier, Antoine. *Comme disait M. de Tocqueville.* Paris, 1925.

Rémond, René. *Les Etats-Unis devant l'opinion française, 1815–1852.* 2 vols. Paris, 1962.

Rémusat, Charles de. *Mémoires de ma vie.* 4 vols. Paris, 1958–1962.

Richter, Melvin. "Comparative Political Analysis in Montesquieu and Tocqueville." *Comparative Politics,* I, no. 2 (Jan. 1969), pp. 129–160.

___, ed. *Essays in Theory and History.* Cambridge, Mass., 1970.

___. *The Politics of Conscience. T. H. Green and his Age.* London, 1964.

___. "Tocqueville on Algeria." *Review of Politics,* XXV, no. 3 (1963), pp. 362–398.

Riesman, David. "Tocqueville as Ethnographer." *The American Scholar,* 30, No. 2 (Spring, 1961), pp. 174–187.

Robertson, Roland. *The Sociological Interpretation of Religion.* New York, 1970.

de Ruggiero, Guido. *The History of European Liberalism.* Boston, 1959.

Sainte-Beuve, Charles Augustin. *Nouveaux Lundis.* Paris, 1868.

Salomon, Albert. "Tocqueville, Moralist and Sociologist." *Social Research,* II (1935), pp. 405–427.

___. "Tocqueville's Philosophy of Freedom." *Review of Politics,* I (1939), pp. 400–431.

Schleifer, James T. "The Making of Tocqueville's *Democracy:* Studies in the Development of Alexis de Tocqueville's Work on America with Particular Attention to His Sources, His Ideas, and His Methods." Unpublished diss., Yale University, 1972.

Scott, John A. *Republican Ideas and the Liberal Tradition in France, 1870–1914.* New York, 1951.

Seignobos, Charles. *La Révolution de 1848—le second empire.* Paris, 1921.

Shackleton, Robert. *Montesquieu.* London, 1961.

Simpson, F. A. *Louis Napoleon and the Recovery of France.* London, 1951.

Smith, James Ward, and Jamison, A. Leland, eds. *The Shaping of American Religion.* Princeton, 1961.

138

Soltau, Roger. *French Political Thought in the 19th Century.* New York, 1959.

Spencer, Philip. *Politics of Belief in Nineteenth-Century France.* New York, 1954.

Spitzer, Alan B. "The Good Napoleon III." *French Historical Studies,* II, no. 3 (Spring 1962), pp. 308–329.

_____. *Old Hatreds and Young Hopes. The French Carbonari Against the Bourbon Restoration.* Cambridge, Mass., 1971.

Strout, Cushing. "Tocqueville's Duality: Describing America and Thinking of Europe." *American Quarterly,* XXI, no. 1 (Spring 1969), pp. 87–99.

Swart, Koenraad W. *The Sense of Decadence in Nineteenth-Century France.* The Hague, 1964.

Sweet, William Warren. *Religion in the Development of American Culture, 1765–1840.* New York, 1952.

Swetchine, Sophie. *Lettres inédites.* Edited by Alfred de Falloux. Paris, 1866.

Sylvain, Robert. "Relations d'Alexis de Tocqueville avec les Catholiques américains." *Revue de l'Université de Laval,* XI (Feb. 1957), pp. 471–486.

Thompson, J. M. *Louis-Napoleon and the Second Empire.* Oxford, 1954.

Thureau-Dangin, Paul. *L'Eglise et l'Etat sous la Monarchie de Juillet.* Paris, 1880.

Tudesq, André-Jean. *Les grands notables en France (1840–1849).* 2 vols. Paris, 1964.

Vacherot, Etienne. *La Démocratie.* Paris, 1860.

Vidler, Alec R. *Prophecy and Papacy.* New York, 1954.

Vigier, Philippe. *La Seconde République dans la région Alpine.* 2 vols. Paris, 1964.

Virtanen, Reino. "Tocqueville and the Romantics." *Symposium,* XIII, no. 2 (Fall 1959), pp. 167-185.

Wach, Joachim. "The Role of Religion in the Social Philosophy of Alexis de Tocqueville." *Journal of the History of Ideas,* VII, no. 1 (Jan. 1946), pp. 74–90.

Walzer, Michael. *The Revolution of the Saints.* New York, 1970.

Weill, Georges. *Histoire du Catholicisme libéral en France, 1828–1908.* Paris, 1909.

_____. *Histoire de l'enseignement secondaire en France.* Paris, 1921.

_____. *Histoire de l'idée laïque en France au XIXe siècle.* Paris, 1929.

White, Hayden. *Metahistory. The Historical Imagination in Nineteenth-Century Europe.* Baltimore, 1973.

Wolin, Sheldon S. *Politics and Vision.* Boston, 1960.

Woodward, E. L. *Three Studies in European Conservatism.* London, 1929.

Zeldin, Theodore, ed. *Conflicts in French Society.* London, 1970.

Zeldin, Theodore. *France 1848–1945.* Vol. I. Oxford, 1973.

Zetterbaum, Marvin. *Tocqueville and the Problem of Democracy.* Stanford, 1967.

Index

Lamoricière, General de, 69
legitimism, 32, 48, 53, 65, 67, 84
Lesueur, Abbé, 1, 2, 11
liberal Catholicism, 34–36, 91n., 129;
  during Second Empire, 84–88
Lipset, Seymour M., 25
Louis Napoleon, 9, 31, 59, 61, 62, 65,
  67, 69, 84, 85, 86, 87; coup d'état,
  81–82; and freedom of teaching,
  63–64; and Roman Affair,
  70–71, 73–74, 75

materialism, 4–5, 37, 52, 88, 89, 90,
  110, 128
Melun, Armand de, 52–53, 61–62
Memoir on Pauperism (*Mémoire sur le
  paupérisme*; Tocqueville; 1835)
  51–52
Merton, Robert, 126
Michelet, Jules, 43, 51
Mill, John Stuart, 1, 5
Miller, Perry, 25–26
Mohammed, *see* Islam
Montalembert, Charles de, 35–36, 43,
  46, 48, 64, 68, 70, 72, 81, 84, 85,
  86, 87. *See also* freedom of teach-
  ing *and* liberal Catholicism
Montesquieu, Charles de, 9, 11, 16, 34,
  94, 112; and comparative study
  of religion, 101–103
Muslims, *see* Islam
Musset, Alfred de, 4. *See also* roman-
  ticism

Ozanam, Fréderic, 49, 53, 58. *See also*
  social Catholicism during July
  Monarchy

Parieu, Esquirou de, 67–68. *See also*
  freedom of teaching during
  Second Republic
Pascal, Blaise, 8n., 10–11
penal reform in France, 40–41

Pierson, George Wilson, 3, 16, 123
Pius IX, 84, 85, 86; and Roman
  Revolution of 1848, 70–74. *See
  also* liberal Catholicism during
  Second Empire *and* Ultramontanism
political conservatism, Tocqueville
  and, 124, 126–127, 131
political liberalism, Tocqueville and,
  124, 126–127, 131
political participation, and religion,
  128
Prévost-Paradol, Lucien, 129
Protestantism: in England, 34,
  103–105; in France, 109–110; in
  United States, 19–22, 25–26, 102

Providence, 121–123, 130
public assistance: during July Monarchy, 52; during Second
  Republic, 60–62. *See also*
  socialism
public morality, and Catholic clergy,
  90–93; Christianity and, 37, 88,
  89, 91–96; and democratization,
  88, 90, 95; and Hinduism, 113;
  during July Monarchy, 89; political participation and, 89, 90,
  128; Revolution of 1848 and,
  89–90; in United States, 88–89
public spirit, *see* public morality
public virtue, *see* public morality

Quinet, Edgar, 43

racial theories, 4, 12, 113
Ranke, Leopold von, 122
Reeve, Henry, 72n., 85
Rémond, René, 15
Rémusat, Charles de, 50, 63, 68
Renouvier, Charles, 129
Restoration, 2–3, 15, 16, 17, 22, 32, 34

143